Howard Crosby

Expository Notes on the Book of Joshua

Volume 1

Howard Crosby

Expository Notes on the Book of Joshua
Volume 1

ISBN/EAN: 9783348023382

Printed in Europe, USA, Canada, Australia, Japan

Cover: Foto ©Lupo / pixelio.de

More available books at **www.hansebooks.com**

EXPOSITORY NOTES

ON THE BOOK OF

JOSHUA.

BY

HOWARD CROSBY,

PASTOR OF THE FOURTH AVENUE PRESBYTERIAN CHURCH, NEW
YORK, AND CHANCELLOR OF THE UNIVERSITY OF THE
CITY OF NEW YORK.

NEW YORK:

ROBERT CARTER AND BROTHERS,

530 BROADWAY.

1875.

Cambridge :
Press of John Wilson & Son.

PREFACE.

THE Book of Joshua records the conquest of Canaan by the children of Israel, and their permanent establishment in the land. Although the destructive criticism has attempted to disprove its unity, its arguments have been specious and puerile. No book of the Scriptures is more consistent with itself, and is more well-proportioned and complete in its construction. It opens with God's order to Joshua, as Moses' successor, to lead Israel into Canaan, and it closes with Joshua's death, after the conquest and settlement of the country under his leadership had been sealed by twenty years of peaceful possession.

In a few places there are indications of omissions, where it is likely parts of the book have failed in the transcription; but these occur in geographical lists, where such omissions would be most apt to occur, and where they are of least importance. Examples of such omissions are in chap. xv., between the fifty-ninth and sixtieth verses, where a group of prominent towns of Judah are wanting (though given in the LXX), and in the description of Manasseh's border in chap. xvii. The narrative, though regular in its order, sometimes, it is true, mentions an incident out of its chronological place, but in such cases forms the exception for the sake of the continuity of another chain of events. Neither the omissions nor these occasional departures from an annalist's chronological exactness invalidate in the slightest the perfect unity of the book; and therefore from this argument no ground is gained against its authenticity as a work composed very soon after the events it records, perhaps by Phinehas the high-priest. All attempts to find a later date from the character of the Hebrew used in the book are equally vain, the language being precisely that which we should expect to follow the Mosaic period, and presenting no difficulty whatever to the comparative linguist.

That the book was written shortly after the events which it records, is evident from chap. vi. 25, where Rahab is spoken of as still living in the writer's time.

The book naturally divides itself into two parts: the conquest of the land, and the distribution of its districts to the tribes. Each of these divisions occupies twelve chapters of the twenty-four. In composing the book, doubtless public records prepared by Joshua and by Eleazer were used; and to this fact may be attributed such repetitions as that of the phrase, " the land had rest from war," in chap. xi. 23, and chap. xiv. 15, and such gaps as those between chap. xxii. and xxiii., and between chap. xxiii. and xxiv., only such selections being made as were appropriate to a *people's book*, that should be in constant use among the tribes.

The two general divisions of the book, the one touching the conquest and the other touching the distribution, may be subdivided as follows:—

I. Joshua's encouragement, chap. i. 1–9.
II. Joshua's preliminary preparations for crossing Jordan, chap. i. 10—ii. 24.
III. Joshua's ultimate preparations for crossing Jordan, chap. iii. 1–13.
IV. The crossing, chap. iii. 14–v. 1.
V. Preparations for the conquest, chap. v. 2–vi.
VI. The conquest, chap. vii.–xii.
VII. The inheritance of the two tribes and a half, chap. xiii.
VIII. The inheritance of the nine tribes and a half, chap. xiv.–xix.
IX. The cities of refuge, chap. xx.
X. The Levitical cities, chap. xxi.
XI. The return of the two tribes and a half, chap. xxii.
XII. Joshua's two farewell addresses, chap. xxiii.–xxiv.

The present little volume is an attempt to put in succinct form such explanations of the text as may help the reader to its clearer understanding, without annoying him with the details of criticism. For a thorough topographical examination of the Book of Joshua, one should use the maps of Robinson or Van de Velde, or the newly published and very valuable maps found in Smith's Ancient Atlas.

Not wishing to burden the notes with discussion, I have put in an Appendix such thoughts on some of the main points of the history as I wished to express at greater length.

In the hope that this effort may contribute its little to the extension of Bible knowledge, and to the blessed fruits of such knowledge, I submit it to its readers.

-H. C.

COMMENTARY ON JOSHUA.

CHAPTER I.

I. JOSHUA'S ENCOURAGEMENT. (Ver. 1–9.)

1 Now after the death of Moses, the servant of the LORD, it came to pass, that the LORD spake unto Joshua the son of Nun, Moses' minister, saying,

THIS passage is the connecting link between Deuteronomy and the book of Joshua. It presents Joshua taking the place of Moses by the Divine command.

VER. 1. *Moses the servant of the Lord.* Moses has this high designation given him in the Scriptures far oftener than any other man (Ex. xiv. 31; Num. xii. 7; Deut. xxxiv. 5; Josh. ix. 24; 1 Kings viii. 56; 2 Kings xviii. 12; 2 Kings xxi. 8; 1 Chron. vi. 49; 2 Chron. xxiv. 9; Neh. x. 29; Dan. ix. 11; Mal. iv. 4; Rev. xv. 3; Ps. cv. 26). The ground of this peculiar emphasis may be found (Num. xii. 8, and Heb. iii. 5) in Moses' singular faithfulness. The title "servant of God" is also applied in Scripture to patriarchs, as Abraham, Jacob, and Job; to prophets, as Elijah, Jonah,

1*

Daniel, and Isaiah ; to a pious king, as Hezekiah ;
to a good leader, as Zerubbabel ; to an upright
statesman, as Eliakim, in Hezekiah's time ; to apos-
tles, as Paul and James and John ; and even to a
heathen monarch, as Nebuchadnezzar. May the
application in the last case be an indication that
Nebuchadnezzar became a true child of God by
faith ?

Spake unto. By Urim and Thummim. (See latter part of the next note.)

Joshua, the son of Nun, was of the tribe of
Ephraim, and first appears as generalissimo of the
army of Israel (as distinguished from the " children
of Israel" at large), in the battle against the Amalekites near Rephidim (Ex. xviii. 9). He was
then over forty years of age, according to Josephus
(Ant. v. 1, 29). At Mount Sinai he was the
special attendant upon Moses (Ex. xxiv. 13, xxxii.
17, xxxiii. 11), holding a position near him during
the first forty days' separation on the mount, and
also afterward in the provisional tabernacle. He
next appears as, in conjunction with Caleb, oppos-
ing the cowardly report of ten of the spies who
had been sent to view the land of Canaan (Num.
xiv. 6). Thirty-eight years later, God orders his
special appointment as the successor of Moses
(Num. xxvii. 18). He was to be to Eleazar what
Moses had been to Aaron. Yet Joshua never had
the high distinction which Moses had of having
the Lord talk to him " mouth to mouth " (Num.
xii. 8). The phraseology in Num. xxvii. 20 shows

2 Moses my servant is dead; now therefore arise, go over this Jordan, thou and all this people, unto the land which I do give to them, *even* to the children of Israel.

3 Every place that the sole of your foot shall tread upon, that have I given unto you, as I said unto Moses.

Joshua's inferiority to Moses, as well as the fact that he was directed to apply to the Urim and Thummim of the high-priest for direction, whereas Moses went directly to the Lord.

Joshua is here called " *Moses' minister ;* " that is, " Moses' attendant," indicative of his previous position before the people.

VER. 2. *Moses my servant is dead.* Yet we see Moses with Jesus on the mount of transfiguration fifteen centuries afterward. There is no death for the servant of God (John xi. 26). It cannot be too much insisted upon that our common use of the word " death " has relation only to a semblance and type of death, to wit, the dissolution of the body, and the soul's departure from it (2 Cor. v. 8), while the only true death, the death intended in Gen. ii. 17, is the dreadful departure of the soul from God.

Go over this Jordan. There is here a double definition of Israel's future possession that should be carefully noted. First, there is the land beyond the Jordan, that is, between the Jordan and the Mediterranean Sea, which was the land originally promised to Abraham (Gen. xii. 7).

Then, secondly, there is the larger territory, " *Every place that the sole of your foot shall tread upon, that have I given you, as I said unto Moses,* (*i.e.*, in Ex. xxiii. 31), *from the wilderness and this Lebanon even unto the great river, the river Euphrates, all the land of the Hittites, and unto the great sea toward the going down of the sun.*" This second definition takes in the whole country from the Euphrates to the Mediterranean, a territory six times as large as the tract between the Jordan and the sea. The smaller tract, which we call Palestine or Canaan, was to be, so to speak, the " adytum," or sacred centre of the holy nation, while, according to their faith and faithfulness, they should extend their sway to the limits of the larger district, southward to the Red Sea, and northward and eastward to the Euphrates. The latter boundaries were reached in the days of David and Solomon. Joshua was simply to lead Israel into their central home, where they were all to be settled, except the tribes of Reuben and Gad, and the half tribe of Manasseh. These were to settle east of the Jordan, by a permission granted to their earnestness of petition, and not according to the original command of God. A careful reading of Numbers xxxii. will show that this exceptional treatment of Reuben, Gad, and one half Manasseh, was, like the establishment of the kingdom afterward (1 Sam. viii. 7), and the building of the temple (2 Sam. vii. 7), an action not ordered by God, but permitted to the importunity of the people. All these three actions proved disastrous. The settlement of Reuben, Gad, and one half Manasseh east of Jordan exposed them to early

4 From the wilderness and this Lebanon even unto
the great river, the river Euphrates, all the land of the
Hittites, and unto the great sea toward the going down
of the sun, shall be your coast.

injury from enemies and broke up the national
unity, the establishment of the kingdom made the
people to seek foreign alliances and introduce foreign manners, and the building of the temple
turned their religion from its simple channels into
a pompous and gorgeous externalism, encouraging
wealth and display among the people, and destroying the heart-piety of the nation.

VER. 4. *This Lebanon.* Lebanon (strictly Anti-
Lebanon, yet the same system of mountains) was
in sight from the camp at Shittim. Hence the
demonstrative "this." [It is possible that "this"
may refer to the desert and Lebanon as one line.]
The line from the desert, say at Akabah on the
Red Sea to Lebanon, north and south, is taken as
a base line, and then the country east to the Euphrates is given, and afterward that west to the
sea. It is the former (from the base line to the
Euphrates) that is called *the land of the Hittites.*
It is true that some Hittites lived west of the Jordan (Gen. xxiii. 3), but the bulk of this important
people dwelt between Damascus and the Euphrates, as we find by the lately discovered chronicles
of the Assyrian monarchs. They are spoken of as
the *Khatti*, a formidable people against whom the
first Tiglath Pileser (about B.C. 1130) waged war.
Their territory, it is probable, extended at one
time as far east as Lake Urumiyeh. They were,

5 There shall not any man be able to stand before thee all the days of thy life: as I was with Moses, *so* I will be with thee : I will not fail thee, nor forsake thee.

6 Be strong and of a good courage: for unto this people shalt thou divide for an inheritance the land which I sware unto their fathers to give them.

doubtless, the most warlike, formidable, and extended of all the Canaanitish races. In the Egyptian records we find them in the time of Sethos (say B.C. 1325) near the Orontes.

VER. 5. *There shall not any man be able to stand before thee*, &c. The promise, given (Deut. xi. 25) to all the people as God's holy nation, is here given to Joshua as its head. So also the words, used to all Israel by Moses (Deut. xxxi. 6), and afterward to Joshua personally (Deut. xxxi. 8), are here repeated to Joshua for his encouragement. The apostle shows (Heb. xiii. 5) that every child of God may apply such a promise directly to himself. The principles of God's government are always the same, however much the local details may change.

VER. 6. *Be strong and of a good courage.* There is very little difference in the meanings of these two words. We might refer the former to strength, and the latter to the firm stand which is the result of strength. We should be led to suppose from the repetition of these words that Joshua was by nature timid or diffident (Deut. xxxi. 7, 23 ; Josh. i. 6, 7, 9). The immense responsibility, now placed upon his shoulders through the death of Moses, began to be felt.

7 Only be thou strong and very courageous, that thou mayest observe to do according to all the law which Moses my servant commanded thee: turn not from it *to* the right hand or *to* the left, that thou mayest prosper whithersoever thou goest.

8 This book of the law shall not depart out of thy mouth; but thou shalt meditate therein day and night, that thou mayest observe to do according to all that is written therein: for then thou shalt make thy way prosperous, and then thou shalt have good success.

9 Have not I commanded thee? Be strong and of a good courage; be not afraid, neither be thou dismayed: for the LORD thy God *is* with thee whithersoever thou goest.

10 ¶ Then Joshua commanded the officers of the people, saying,

VER. 7–9. It would require strength and courage to observe strictly God's law before so great a people, and then again a strict observance of that law would make him prosperous and wise in action. It is no cursory look at God's written word that is required, but *a meditating therein day and night* (comp. Ps. i. 2), that needs the courage and confers the success. Fear and dismay at one's enemies are for ever gone under this spiritual regimen.

II. JOSHUA'S PRELIMINARY PREPARATIONS FOR CROSSING JORDAN. (Ver. 10–18, and chap. ii. 1–24.)

1. *General Orders.*

VER. 10. *The officers of the people.* The people of Israel had officers (shoterim) over them when in Egypt (Ex. v. 6, 19). From Num. xi. 16, we gather they were elders also, men selected in each tribe and family for their years and experience. The "seventy" (Num. l. c.) were selected from

11 Pass through the host and command the people, saying, Prepare you victuals; for within three days ye shall pass over this Jordan, to go in to possess the land which the LORD your God giveth you to possess it.

12 ¶ And to the Reubenites, and to the Gadites, and to half the tribe of Manasseh, spake Joshua, saying,

these as the special assessors of Moses. In the semi-patriarchal condition of Israel, these men were probably recognized without any uniform method of election. Joshua moves the great host through their agency.

VER. 11. *Pass through the host.* Lit., " Pass over in the middle of the camp." It implies personal contact with all parts of the vast host.

Victuals. Heb., " zedah," which is *food for a journey.* On the sixteenth day of Nisan the manna, that had been their miraculous food for forty years, was to cease (chap. v. 12). Between that time and their *full* supply from the land of Canaan there would be an interval of *scant* supply. This present provision was for that emergency. If this order was given on the seventh of Nisan, it was given more than a week before the manna ceased, and would be a token of that coming fact, and, in the sequel, a helper to their faith. The verse may, therefore, be thus paraphrased : " Prepare you victuals, for in a few days you shall cross Jordan and enter your own land, where the manna, your wilderness-bread, shall cease, and you will need your own prepared supply." This preparation of victuals was thus itself an exercise of their faith.

13 Remember the word which Moses the servant of the LORD commanded you, saying, The LORD your God hath given you rest, and hath given you this land.

Within three days. They crossed on the tenth day of Nisan (chap. iv. 19). Hence this order is given on the seventh of the month. As the spies returned to the camp before the people crossed (chap. ii. 23), and as these spies had been three days (*i.e.*, parts of three days) in the mountain west of Jordan (chap. ii. 22), they must have been sent out by Joshua on the sixth of the month, although the story of their expedition is not given until after this account of the command issued on the seventh.

Which the Lord your God giveth you to possess it. Lit., " Jehovah your God." It is important that Israel should bear in mind, at the very beginning of their occupation of the land, that they did not possess it in their own right or by their own might, but received it as a gift from God. This is the true basis of all human possession, a knowledge of which will tend to make us humble and satisfied.

VER. 13. *The word which Moses the servant of the Lord commanded you.* The record is found in Num. xxxii. 20–28, and Deut. iii. 18–20. It was necessary to remind the two and a half tribes of the arrangement made ; for the same love of ease which prompted them at first to ask for the land east of Jordan, might tempt them to be lax in keeping their engagement to help their brethren.

This land, i.e., the land on which Joshua stood when he spake, east of the Jordan.

B

14 Your wives, your little ones, and your cattle shall remain in the land which Moses gave you on this side Jordan; but ye shall pass before your brethren armed, all the mighty men of valour, and help them;

15 Until the LORD have given your brethren rest, as *he hath given* you, and they also have possessed the land which the LORD your God giveth them: then ye shall return unto the land of your possession, and enjoy it, which Moses the LORD's servant gave you on this side Jordan toward the sun-rising.

VER. 14. *On this side Jordan.* Lit., "beyond Jordan." (See on ver. 15.)

Armed. A peculiar Hebrew word, used of Israel at the exodus (Ex. xiii. 18), and also in Josh. iv. 12, and Judges vii. 11, and supposed by some to mean "arranged in ranks of five," but better understood as meaning primarily "girded."

All the mighty men of valour. That is, all who could be spared from the equally necessary duty of protecting the wives, little ones, and cattle on the east side. In chap. iv. 13, we see that forty thousand of these two and a half tribes passed over; but from Num. xxxvi. 7, 18, 34, we find that the warriors of these tribes were 110,580; so that over seventy thousand must have remained to guard their country. This was not consulting their ease, and hence was no breach of their contract. Yet the necessity of leaving seventy thousand warriors behind may be quoted as one of the evils attending upon their original desire to settle outside of Canaan.

VER. 15. *On this side Jordan toward the sunrising.* Lit., "*Beyond* Jordan toward the sunrising," *i.e.*, beyond, as viewed from the promised land.

16 ¶ And they answered Joshua saying, All that thou commandest us, we will do, and whithersoever thou sendest us, we will go.

17 According as we hearkened unto Moses in all things, so will we hearken unto thee: only the LORD thy God be with thee, as he was with Moses.

18 Whosoever *he be* that doth rebel against thy commandment, and will not hearken unto thy words in all that thou commandest him, he shall be put to death: only be strong and of a good courage.

VER. 16–18. These two and a half tribes show a very praiseworthy zeal, and a desire to sustain the courage of Joshua. (See note on ver. 6.) They were faithful to their word. (See chap. xxii. 1–6.)

CHAPTER II.

2. *The Spies.*

1 AND Joshua the son of Nun sent out of Shittim
two men to spy secretly, saying, Go view the land,
even Jericho. And they went, and came into an harlot's house, named Rahab, and lodged there.

VER. 1. *Shittim.*   The full name is (Num.
xxxiii. 49) Abel-hash-Shittim.   The shittah is a
species of acacia-tree, of which several varieties
are found in Egypt and the neighboring lands.
Abel-hash-Shittim is literally " meadow of the aca-
cias."   From these acacia-trees the gum-arabic is
obtained.   The Arabs give the name of Seyal to
the species which is most abundant in the Palestine region.   It is a thorny tree and grows in thick-
·ets.   The place *Shittim* doubtless derived its name
from their abundance.   Shittim was situated on
the east side of the Arabah (Num. xxii. 1, *Arboth
Moab*, or " plains of Moab "), close under the Moab
mountains, probably at the *debouchure* of the
Wady Hesban into the plain, about five miles from
the Jordan.   The Arabah (now El-Ghor) is here
about thirteen miles wide, the eastern heights averaging five miles, and the western averaging eight
miles from the river.   Under the mountains the
plain is green, and was probably more so in ancient

times; but out toward the river it is dry and sterile, except where the dense verdure along the course of the Jordan itself makes an exception. Shittim was the head-quarters of the host of Israel during the attempt of Balak to curse Israel. (Comp. Num. xxii. 1, and xxv. 1.) They doubtless abode there a long time, to rest and prepare the host after the contests with Sihon, with Og, and with the Midianites. It was from Shittim that Moses went up to the top of Pisgah and died (Deut. xxxiv. 1). In Num. xxxiii. 49, we find that the encampment stretched from Beth-jesimoth to Shittim. Now if Beth-jesimoth is rightly placed by Kiepert, Van de Velde, and others near the spot where the Jordan enters the Dead Sea, then the host of Israel may be considered as occupying all the south side of Wady Hesban from the hills to Jordan, a distance of five miles, their more compact desert order being altered for the emergency.

Two men. Two, for mutual counsel and support. The Saviour sent out his disciples two and two. One of these men was probably Salmon, the son of Nahshon, prince of Judah, who afterward married Rahab. (See Num. ii. 3, Ruth iv. 20, and Matt. i. 5.) It is likely that the spies would be taken from the leading men of Israel, as in the former instance, thirty-eight years previously; and Salmon's probable age would agree with the statement that these spies were young men (Josh. vi. 23).

To spy secretly. The words in Hebrew are "spies, secretly saying." That is, Joshua gave

2 And it was told the king of Jericho, saying, Behold, there came men in hither to-night of the children
of Israel, to search out the country.

them secret instructions, not letting the host know
aught about it, lest they might spread information
of the fact to the marring of the plan.

The land, even Jericho. Rather, " the land and
Jericho." They were especially to inspect Jericho,
but also to notice the condition of the land generally. Jericho lay about six miles west of the Jordan, near the prolific fountain of Ain es-Sultan.

A harlot's house. Their going to such a house
would prevent observation, they might suppose.
And, moreover, it was probably very near the gate
they entered, for we know the house was partly
built on the town-wall (Josh. ii. 15).

VER. 2. *The king of Jericho.* From the enumeration in chap. xii. we see there were at least thirty-
one kings in Canaan. This would not give a
territory much over ten miles square to each.
The king of Jericho would naturally hold sway over
the lower Jordan valley, west of the river, his
territory being bounded on the west by the limestone heights, of which Kuruntul is most conspicuous. The region near the fountain is to-day very
green and fertile. A few Arab houses, and a ruined
castle called Eriha or Er-Riha, may be considered
the sorry representation of the famous Jericho.

Behold, there came men in hither to-night. The
speed with which the news reached the king
shows, what we should naturally expect, that the

3 And the king of Jericho sent unto Rahab, saying, Bring forth the men that are come to thee, which are entered into thine house: for they be come to search out all the country.

4 And the woman took the two men, and hid them, and said thus, There came men unto me, but I wist not whence they *were:*

5 And it came to pass *about the time* of shutting of the gate, when it was dark, that the men went out: whither the men went, I wot not: pursue after them quickly; for ye shall overtake them.

greatest vigilance was used against the vast host of Israelites that threatened the border. A great terror had seized upon the Canaanitish kings, as they knew that this strange and numerous people, who had for forty years been dwelling in the southern desert, and regarding whom they had heard such stories of wonder, was about to move upon them and invade their land. (See ver. 9–11.) The only safety could be in the most thorough vigilance.

VER. 3. *For they be come to search out all the country.* The king takes for granted that Rahab is ignorant of the true object of the two men, and is therefore wholly unprepared for her ruse. This makes her task the easier.

VER. 4, 5. *I wist not,* &c. Rahab's lie is not to be defended. She was ignorant of the moral iniquity of a lie, as she was probably of that of her own style of life. The depravity of Canaan had certainly lowered the standard of morality in the minds of all; but this should not lead us to justify Rahab, however much the flagrancy of her offence be modified. God regarded her faith and overlooked her lie, as in the case of Jael.

6 But she had brought them up to the roof of the house, and hid them with the stalks of flax, which she had laid in order upon the roof.

7 And the men pursued after them the way to Jordan unto the fords: and as soon as they which pursued after them were gone out, they shut the gate.

VER. 6. *Hid them with the stalks of flax.* Lit., "buried them in the flax of wood." The word translated "hid" is entirely different from the word so translated in the fourth verse. This verb, *taman*, signifies a hiding by putting down under something. On the house-top (the flat roof of an oriental house) Rahab had piles of *woody flax*, or flax-stalks, and under these she put the two young men.

VER. 7. *The men*, i.e., the messengers of the king.

The way to Jordan unto the fords. The Jordan has several fording-places over against Jericho, all of which, however, are impassable when the river is full. At this time the river *was* full (chap. iii. 15). Hence, we may suppose the Jericho people felt tolerably secure against any immediate attack from the Israelites. The Arabs swim across the river; but, owing to the great swiftness of the current, it is not an easy matter. Swimming across for an armed host would be impossible. The river is from eighty to one hundred feet wide at this part.

They shut the gate. A mark of time. (Comp. ver. 5.) The time of gate-shutting would naturally be when day-light was entirely past, say at seven o'clock in the evening at the season indicated in

8 ¶ And before they were laid down, she came up
unto them upon the roof;
9 And she said unto the men, I know that the LORD
hath given you the land, and that your terror is fallen
upon us, and that all the inhabitants of the land faint
because of you.

the narrative. Rahab had represented the young
men as leaving *about* gate-shutting time, that is,
just before the messengers arrived. The messengers hurry away, and pass out the gate *exactly* at
gate-shutting. Jericho may have had only one gate
(like Osiout, the capital of Upper Egypt, to-day);
or "the gate" may mean the particular gate in
question, *i.e.*, that on the side toward the Jordan.

VER. 8. *Laid down*, *i.e.*, to sleep, after leaving
their hiding-place under the flax. They would lie
down to sleep on the flat roof, according to oriental
custom.

VER. 9. *I know that the Lord.* Lit., "I know
that Jehovah." Rahab here shows that she had
watched the course of God with Israel, and had
been convinced that Israel's God, Jehovah, was the
only true God, and had prepared her heart for his
providential dealings, which now meet her in
mercy. Her description of the effect of Israel's
history upon the people of Canaan gives us a
graphic idea of the consternation which the stupendous facts of Israel's wilderness life had produced upon surrounding nations. The people of
Canaan especially were agitated, as they knew that
they would be the direct objects of attack.

Faint. Heb., "melt," as in Ex. xv. 15. So in
2

10 For we have heard how the LORD dried up the water of the Red sea for you, when ye came out of Egypt; and what ye did unto the two kings of the Amorites that *were* on the other side Jordan, Sihon and Og, whom ye utterly destroyed.

11 And as soon as we had heard *these things*, our hearts did melt, neither did there remain any more courage in any man, because of you: for the LORD your God, he *is* God in heaven above, and in earth beneath.

12 Now therefore, I pray you, swear unto me by the LORD, since I have shewed you kindness, that ye will also shew kindness unto my father's house, and give me a true token:

13 And *that* ye will save alive my father, and my mother, and my brethren, and my sisters, and all that they have, and deliver our lives from death.

ver. 24. Comp. chap. vii. 5, for the fuller expression, but with another Hebrew verb. It betokens extreme discouragement.

VER. 10. The two events that signalized the beginning and the end of Israel's course from Egypt to Canaan are mentioned by Rahab as equally well known to the Canaanites. Doubtless all between was also well known.

VER. 11. *Melt.* A different Hebrew word from that translated "faint" in ver. 9, but having about the same signification.

Courage. Lit., "breath" or "life."

For the Lord your God, he is God. This is not the conclusion the Canaanites came to, but that to which Rahab came. She argued from Israel's guidance and from Canaan's fear.

VER. 12. Rahab's request shows her perfect confidence in the taking of Jericho by Israel, and also her tender regard for her own kindred. Her faith

14 And the men answered her, Our life for yours, if ye utter not this our business. And it shall be, when the LORD hath given us the land, that we will deal kindly and truly with thee.

15 Then she let them down by a cord through the window: for her house *was* upon the town-wall, and she dwelt upon the wall.

16 And she said unto them, Get you to the mountain, lest the pursuers meet you; and hide yourselves there three days, until the pursuers be returned: and afterward may ye go your way.

in Jehovah had, doubtless, revived affections that her course of life may have marred.

A true token. Lit., " a sign of truth," *i.e.,* a promise under oath, which would assure her of its truth, and make her confident of their faithfulness.

VER. 14. *If ye utter not this our business.* That is, " if ye make not known the object of our visit."

Deal kindly and truly with thee. Lit., " do to thee mercy and truth;" *i.e.,* do thee the favor asked and keep our pledge.

VER. 15. This anticipates verses 16–21, for we cannot suppose the conversation there given occurred while she was at the window and the men below on the ground.

VER. 16. *The mountain* would be Kuruntul or Quarantana, only two miles away westward. This mountain rises precipitously from the plain, a wall of rock, twelve hundred feet high, full of caverns, in some one of which the spies may have hid themselves. The mountain gets its present name from a late tradition that it was the scene of our Lord's forty days' fasting.

17 And the men said unto her, We *will be* blameless of this thine oath which thou hast made us swear.

18 Behold, *when* we come into the land, thou shalt bind this line of scarlet thread in the window which thou didst let us down by: and thou shalt bring thy father, and thy mother, and thy brethren, and all thy father's household home unto thee.

19 And it shall be, *that* whosoever shall go out of the doors of thy house into the street, his blood *shall be* upon his head, and we *will be* guiltless: and whosoever shall be with thee in the house, his blood *shall be* on our head, if *any* hand be upon him.

20 And if thou utter this our business, then we will be quit of thine oath which thou hast made us to swear.

21 And she said, According unto your words, so *be* it. And she sent them away, and they departed: and she bound the scarlet line in the window.

Three days. See note on chap. i. 11.

VER. 17. They wish to secure their own word by making the way plain to its performance : only *her* remissness will prevent its accomplishment.

VER. 18. *This line of scarlet thread.* Rather " the cord of this crimson thread," *i.e.*, made of crimson thread. Crimson is a color easily distinguishable at a distance, and therefore would be an appropriate color for the object designed. It was the very cord by which she let them down, as we see by the demonstrative " this." Is the thought, which many have expressed here, too strained, that this crimson cord of salvation, saving both the spies and Rahab's family, represented, in this strangely typical history, the saving blood of our Lord Jesus ? The analogy between this and the paschal blood is observable.

VER. 21. *According unto your words.* She would

22 And they went, and came unto the mountain, and abode there three days, until the pursuers were returned: and the pursuers sought *them* throughout all the way, but found *them* not.

23 ¶ So the two men returned, and descended from the mountain, and passed over, and came to Joshua the son of Nun, and told him all *things* that befell them:

24 And they said unto Joshua, Truly the LORD hath delivered into our hands all the land; for even all the inhabitants of the country do faint because of us.

bind the crimson cord in the window on the wall, visible to Israel's army, as it encamps before the town; she would, moreover, bring her entire family into the house, and she would keep the whole matter a profound secret.

VER. 24. These two spies act, as Caleb and Joshua had done thirty-eight years before (Num. xiii. 30, and xiv. 6-9). They took no note of Jericho's great walls, and of her vigilant king, but of the Lord's preparation for Israel's victory.

CHAPTER III.

III. Joshua's Ultimate Preparations for Crossing Jordan. (Ver. 1–13.)

1 And Joshua rose early in the morning; and they removed from Shittim, and came to Jordan, he and all the children of Israel, and lodged there before they passed over.

Ver. 1. *Early in the morning* of the day after the spies returned, the ninth of Nisan.

Came to Jordan. The host moved from its line on Wady Hesban northward and westward to the river bank opposite Jericho. It was a movement of perhaps six miles for the most distant man in the host. The entire day is taken for this grand preparatory arrangement of two millions of people. At the Jordan they remain in position, and spend the night on the east side. The chronology of these three chapters I take to be this: —

6th Nisan, Spies sent out.
7th ,, Joshua's first command (chap. i. 11).
8th ,, Spies return.
9th ,, Movement from Shittim.
10th ,, Crossing.

By this scheme, the "three days" of chap. i. 11, would be from the seventh to the tenth, and the "three days" of chap. iii. 2, would be the same. The "three days" of chap. ii. 16, 22, would be

2 And it came to pass after three days, that the officers went through the host;

3 And they commanded the people, saying, When ye see the ark of the covenant of the LORD your God, and the priests the Levites bearing it, then ye shall remove from your place, and go after it.

from the sixth to the eighth, the *parts* of three days being in the Orient called by the unqualified phrase "three days." The spies would reach Jericho and leave it on the same day in which they left the camp of Israel.

VER. 2. *After three days.* (See preceding note.) The absence of the article does not (as Keil supposes) preclude the reference to the "three days" of chap. i. 11. Comp. Josh. vi. 3, 14, for a like instance. So also 1 Sam. x. 8, with xiii. 8, and Dan. i. 12, 15.

Officers. (See note on chap. i. 10.) This passing of the officers through the host (see note on chap. i. 11) takes place the evening before the crossing, as we see by ver. 5, after the arrival of the host in position before the river. The orders given through these officers come, of course, from Joshua.

VER. 3. *And they commanded the people.* The one object of this special order was, that the host should be guided by the movement of the ark of the covenant, following it in their regular column at a distance of about a half mile. This may have been the distance usually observed in the wilderness encampments between the tents of Israel (exclusive of Levi) and the tabernacle, but the passage in Num. ii. 2, does not give us the distance, but

4 Yet there shall be a space between you and it, about two thousand cubits by measure: come not near unto it, that ye may know the way by which ye must go; for ye have not passed *this* way heretofore.

5 And Joshua said unto the people, Sanctify yourselves: for to-morrow the LORD will do wonders among you.

only uses the expression, " far off," or, strictly, " over against." The people had been used to follow the pillar of cloud as their guide (Ex. xl. 36, and Num. ix. 17). But now that guide is withdrawn, the desert life being over. The people, therefore, need a special command to regard the ark borne by the priests as their new signal of motion.

The priests the Levites. (See Deut. xvii. 9, xxiv. 8, xxxi. 9, 25, and Jer. xxxiii. 21.) This peculiar expression seems to emphasize the tribal character of the priests as against any attempt at leadership by other tribes.

VER. 4. *Two thousand cubits.* (See preceding note.) This distance was made not as a mark of reverence to the ark, but that the ark might be so far advanced before the host as to be clearly seen by a great number. This reason is given in the text, " Come not near unto it, *that ye may know the way by which ye must go.*"

VER. 5. *Sanctify yourselves.* After the first proclamation, carried through the host by the officers, that Israel should be guided by the movements of the ark, Joshua issues another, for Israel to sanctify itself, in readiness for a special manifestation of divine power on the next day. This sanctification

6 And Joshua spake unto the priests, saying, Take up the ark of the covenant, and pass over before the people. And they took up the ark of the covenant, and went before the people.

7 ¶ And the LORD said unto Joshua, This day will I begin to magnify thee in the sight of all Israel, that they may know that as I was with Moses, *so* I will be with thee.

8 And thou shalt command the priests that bear the ark of the covenant, saying, When ye are come to the brink of the water of Jordan, ye shall stand still in Jordan.

is, of course, a *ritual* sanctification, such as is so constantly intended in the history of the Jewish economy. (For examples, see Ex. xix. 10, 22, 23; Lev. xxvii. 14, 16; Joel ii. 16.) It consisted of certain negative abstinences and positive purificatory rites, all which were, indeed, an emblem of inward purity, but had no necessary essential connection therewith. These rites were calculated to impress the mind and prepare the thoughts of Israel for any peculiar display of the divine glory in their behalf.

VER. 6. Here begins the record of a new day, the tenth of Nisan. Joshua gives the order for the priests with the ark to start, and adds (see ver. 8), " When ye come to the brink of the waters of the Jordan, ye shall stand still at the Jordan." Their standing still would be the signal for the miracle, although Joshua may as yet have been ignorant of the issue.

VER. 7, 8. These parenthetical verses tell us of a second appearance of God to Joshua, probably during the preceding night. The first appearance

2*   c

9 ¶ And Joshua said unto the children of Israel, Come hither, and hear the words of the LORD your God.

had taken place three days before, and is recorded in chap. i. 1–9. These appearances may have been like that recorded in chap. v. 13, when God assumed a human form, or they may have been in dreams. Indeed, we *assume* that they were appearances at all. They may have been. unmistakable suggestions from within, or audible words, or even some form of revelation by Urim and Thummim, of which we know so little. Still the probabilities are in favor of a visible appearance, from the passage above referred to.

In this interview God announces to Joshua that he would put him that day on the same high plane of respect before Israel that Moses had occupied. He was about to perform a stupendous miracle before Israel, under Joshua's guidance, of the same character as that at the Red Sea, which had so manifested both the glory of God and the headship of Moses over the people. The crossing of the Red Sea was to be renewed in the crossing of the Jordan. As yet probably both Joshua and the people supposed they would cross Jordan by fording.

VER. 9. When the priests had started with the ark, to move at least a half mile before Israel should follow, Joshua calls the " children of Israel " together ; that is, he summons their officers and representatives.

10 And Joshua said, Hereby ye shall know that the living God *is* among you, and *that* he will without fail drive out from before you the Canaanites, and the Hittites, and the Hivites, and the Perizzites, and the Girgashites, and the Amorites, and the Jebusites.

11 Behold, the ark of the covenant of the LORD of all the earth passeth over before you into Jordan.

12 Now therefore take you twelve men out of the tribes of Israel, out of every tribe a man.

13 And it shall come to pass, as soon as the soles of the feet of the priests that bear the ark of the LORD, the Lord of all the earth, shall rest in the waters of Jordan, *that* the waters of Jordan shall be cut off *from* the waters that come down from above; and they shall stand upon an heap.

VER. 10–13. A grand evidence of God's guiding presence was to be given them, as was given their fathers at the Red Sea. As they had probably seen the pillar of cloud depart from them, such a new sign was very important to sustain their faith. He points them to the ark already on its way ("passeth over" = "is now passing over" before you to Jordan), and bids them select twelve men to represent the twelve tribes, for a purpose afterward to be disclosed. He further tells them that, when the priests' feet touch the water that has overflowed on the lowest bank, the water of the river shall on one hand stand up as a hill, and the water on the other hand shall run off to the Dead Sea and disappear, thus leaving a dry bed of at least four miles in the river's length.

VER. 10. *The living God.* One who is active in all the works of nature and grace; one who is not dead, like the idols of the heathen, or, we may add, like the *abstractions* of the philosophers and the *forces* of the scientists.

Canaanites, &c. The Canaanites are first mentioned, and the land is called the land of Canaan, because this special tribe bore the old ancestral name. We find from Gen. x. 15, that from Canaan, Ham's son, eleven nations had their origin: the Sidonians, Hittites, Jebusites, Amorites, Girgashites, Hivites, Arkites, Sinites, Arvadites, Zemarites, and Hamathites. Six of these do not appear (by name) in Israel's Canaan ; to wit, the Sidonians, Arkites, Sinites, Arvadites, Zemarites, and Hamathites. The other five we find as in this list in our text ; to wit, the Hittites, Jebusites, Amorites, Girgashites, and Hivites. The *Canaanites* (as a distinct tribe) may have been a mixed tribe, taking the ancestral name. The only tribe of this list not found in the tenth of Genesis is the " Perizzites." These *may be* the same as the Zemarites, as we find a city called Zemaraim in Benjamin (Josh. xviii. 22), and a Mount Zemaraim, probably in the same vicinity (2 Chron. xiii. 4). We also find that the Perizzites occupied this portion of Palestine (Josh. xvii. 15 ; Judg. i. 4, 5).

From Gen. xv. 19, 20, we see that four other tribes occupied, with these Canaanitish tribes, the region between Egypt and the Euphrates; to wit, the Kenites, Kenizzites, Kadmonites, and Rephaim, who may have been Ham's descendants by another son than Canaan, or may have been of an entirely different stock, Turanian for example. Of all these

14 ¶ And it came to pass, when the people removed from their tents to pass over Jordan, and the priests bearing the ark of the covenant before the people;
15 And as they that bear the ark were come unto Jordan, and the feet of the priests that bare the ark were dipped in the brim of the water, (for Jordan overfloweth all his banks all the time of harvest,)

tribes the Hittites seem to have waxed largest and strongest, and to have extended farthest northward and eastward. (See note on chap. i. 4.)

The miraculous crossing of the Jordan was to be God's pledge to the Israelites that they should overcome the seven nations.

VER. 13. *Shall be cut off.* Read this whole passage thus: " The waters of the Jordan shall be cut off, namely, the waters running down from above, and they (*i.e.*, the portion from which these are cut off) shall stand up one heap." (Comp. Ex. xv. 8.)

IV. THE CROSSING. (Ver. 14—chap. v. 1.)

VER. 14. The actual movement of the whole host here begins.

VER. 15. *Jordan overfloweth.* The Jordan has, at this part of its course, three distinct banks. Upon the first or lowest grows a dense thicket of bushes and trees; on the second is but little growth of any kind, and on the third is the desert of the Arabah. The first bank is but a few inches above the water. The second bank is about six feet high. The third bank is fifty feet high. The river is

nearly a hundred feet wide, and about twelve feet
deep. The following outline will help the reader
understand this description.

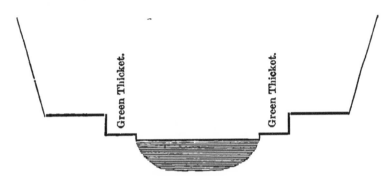

The outer banks are half a mile apart. Here
the proportion in the outline fails. It will be at
once seen by this outline that the entrance of the
ark into the river could not be seen by Israel, for
the high banks would prevent a view. They could
only, as they approached the margin, see the water
gone from the river-bed, and the ark standing in
the middle.

The words translated "overfloweth" mean "fill-
eth upon," and refer to the complete filling up of
the river's bed, so that the water would appear *upon*
the level which we have designated by the words
"green thicket." No greater overflow of the Jordan than this is known. But this overflow * of the
lower level occurs every year in April and May.

* The "swelling of Jordan" mentioned in Jer. xii. 5, xlix. 19,
l. 44, is the same as "the pride of Jordan" in Zech. xi. 3, and
refers not to the waters overflowing, but to the rich green thicket
and foliage of the river banks.

16 That the waters which came down from above stood *and* rose up upon an heap very far from the city Adam, that *is* beside Zaretan; and those that came down toward the sea of the plain, *even* the salt sea, failed, *and* were cut off: and the people passed over right against Jericho.

VER. 16. *Very far from the city Adam.* This should read, " very far off at the city Adam ; " that is, very far from the crossing-place. Of the city *Adam* we know nothing, but Zaretan (or Zeredathah, 2 Chron. iv. 17) is accurately described in 1 K. iv. 12, as near Beth-shean and "under Jezreel." This must fix its position as far north as the Wady Mujeidah, which is forty-four miles north in a straight line from the place of crossing, and twice that distance by the windings of the river. Van de Velde's position at Kurn Sartabeh is entirely too far south. We must suppose that it took the host at least four hours to cross. As the Jordan runs with a current of six miles an hour, and is between ten and twelve feet deep, and as the spot where Wady-Mujeidah enters the Jordan is four hundred and fifty feet higher level than the crossing-place, a stoppage of the Jordan's flow at the crossing-place that would reach in its effects the Wady-Mujeidah would only in the space of four hours make the river three feet deeper for the distance between the two extremities of the disturbance. Thus the wall of water on the north side of the crossing host would be, when at its greatest, but fifteen feet high.

17 And the priests that bare the ark of the covenant of the LORD stood firm on dry ground in the midst of Jordan, and all the Israelites passed over on dry ground, until all the people were passed clean over Jordan.

VER. 17. (Comp. chap. iv. 10.) The ark seems to have taken its station close by the wall of water and in the middle of the river-bed, while the host of Israel passed over below, their right wing being two thousand cubits from the ark (ver. 4). The twelve men chosen from the tribes (ver. 12) would naturally remain somewhere in the vicinity of the ark, awaiting their special orders.

CHAPTER IV.

1 AND it came to pass, when all the people were clean passed over Jordan, that the LORD spake unto Joshua, saying,

2 Take you twelve men out of the people, out of every tribe a man,

VER. 1. *When all the people were clean passed over Jordan.* In the Hebrew style, this *protasis* or preface, while only belonging to ver. 5 and the following verses, is placed before the statement of ver. 1–3. It is idiomatic. We should say, after these words, " the Lord *having spoken* unto Joshua," &c., parenthetically, but the Hebrew uses the finite verb without parenthesis, " that the Lord *spake*," &c., although this command of God to Joshua must have been given before Joshua's command to Israel in ver. 12 of the third chapter, and was probably part of the orders given in the divine interview recorded in chap. iii. 7, 8. It may be that some token was given to Joshua at the time for the accomplishment of this act, and that thus the command was virtually repeated. Such a supposition would account for the words " hence " and " where the priests' feet *stood*," instead of " thence " and " where the priests' feet shall stand," as the phrases would be if the command had been given only before the miracle.

3 And command ye them, saying, Take you hence out of the midst of Jordan, out of the place where the priests' feet stood firm, twelve stones, and ye shall carry them over with you, and leave them in the lodging-place where ye shall lodge this night.

4 Then Joshua called the twelve men, whom he had prepared of the children of Israel, out of every tribe a man:

5 And Joshua said unto them, Pass over before the ark of the LORD your God into the midst of Jordan, and take you up every man of you a stone upon his shoulder, according unto the number of the tribes of the children of Israel:

6 That this may be a sign among you, *that* when your children ask *their fathers* in time to come, saying, What *mean* ye by these stones?

7 Then ye shall answer them, That the waters of Jordan were cut off before the ark of the covenant of the LORD; when it passed over Jordan, the waters of Jordan were cut off: and these stones shall be for a memorial unto the children of Israel for ever.

VER. 3. *Twelve stones.* These were only of such size as that one man could carry each several miles. A rude and small monument was to be made of them.

VER. 4. Now the twelve men are to know why they were selected. (Comp. chap. iii. 12.) They had probably waited on the east bank till now.

VER. 5. *Before the ark,* i.e., to the front of the ark, now standing at the base of the watery wall.

VER. 6. *A sign among you.* A memorial to be preserved in their new country, by which coming generations should be reminded of God's miraculous care and guidance of the people.

In time to come. Lit., " to-morrow."

VER. 7. *These stones shall be for a memorial.* The Oriental custom of throwing up a pile of stones

8 And the children of Israel did so as Joshua commanded, and took up twelve stones out of the midst of Jordan, as the LORD spake unto Joshua, according to the number of the tribes of the children of Israel, and carried them over with them unto the place where they lodged, and laid them down there.

(or erecting one large stone, as the case may be) in commemoration of some important event still prevails, as any traveller in the East has had abundant opportunity to learn. The Scotch " cairn " is of like character, although generally marking a sepulchre rather than an event. For Bible instances like the one in our present passage, see Gen. xxviii. 18, xxxi. 46–48, xxxv. 14; Josh. xxiv. 26; 1 Sam. vii. 12. These stones, thus reared or piled, were counted sacred by the people of a land. A reference to this fact seems to be had in Isa. viii. 14.

VER. 8. *The place where they lodged.* We see from ver. 19 that this was *Gilgal.* Gilgal means a "rolling;" and we are told that this place received its name because the reproach of the new generation of Israel, that they were uncircumcised, was here *rolled* away. (See chap. v. 2–9.) There was another Gilgal six miles north of Bethel, connected with the lives of Elijah and Elisha (2 Kings ii. 2). From the frequent appearance of Jiljilieh (the mod. equivalent) in the modern topography of Palestine, we may see that there were several towns of the name of Gilgal, the name in these other instances referring to the *rolling* character of the ground. The places mentioned in Deut. xi.

9 And Joshua set up twelve stones in the midst of Jordan, in the place where the feet of the priests which bare the ark of the covenant stood: and they are there unto this day.

30, and in Josh. xii. 23, xv. 7, are some of these. Josephus puts the Gilgal of this narrative six miles from the Jordan and one from Jericho. Later writers have put it two, five, and seven miles from Jericho. It is highly probable that it was directly *en route* between the crossing-place of Jordan and Jericho, but whether nearer to the one or the other we have no date to decide. It was probably on the line of Wady Kelt.

Ver. 9. *Set up twelve stones in the midst of Jordan.* Why were these set up where the water of the river would cover them? For with the words, "the midst of Jordan," as repeated seven times (chap. iii. 17, iv. 3, 5, 8, 9, 10, 18), we cannot believe the priests' place of standing with the ark was where they first touched the river (chap. iii. 13), as Keil alleges. The Heb., *bethok*, means "in the middle," and cannot refer to one side or bank of the river. Why, then, were these stones set up where the river would cover them? They could scarcely have formed a monument high enough to overtop the twelve feet of water in the mid-channel, and so to be seen by those on the bank. They were hastily brought together, and probably formed, like those in Gilgal, a mere cairn. As they, therefore, could not be intended to remind the passing generations of the crossing, may

10 ¶ For the priests which bare the ark stood in the midst of Jordan, until every thing was finished that the LORD commanded Joshua to speak unto the people, according to all that Moses commanded Joshua: and the people hasted and passed over.

11 And it came to pass, when all the people were

we not believe that their use is yet in the future, and that they may yet be laid bare as testimony to the minute accuracy of this Old Testament history? Have not Nineveh, Babylon, and their sister-cities been made by God's providence to do this same work?

They are there unto this day, *i.e.*, the day of the writing. (Comp. Judg. i. 26.) There is no proof in the phrase, that it was *well known* at the day of writing. From chap. vi. 25, we may consider " this day " as not more than fifty years after the occurrence, perhaps much earlier.

VER. 10. *According to all that Moses commanded Joshua.* We are nowhere told that Moses gave any commands to Joshua regarding the details of the crossing of Jordan. The phrase refers to the general submission of Joshua to the divine direction, and of the people to Joshua, in accordance with the command of Moses (Deut. xxxi. 3, 7).

Hasted. The movement was a rapid one. God's miraculous works are connected with the rational use of man's faculties. The people were not to abuse God's favor by carelessness or delay. Their celerity of movement was a token of their co-operation with God's favor, in the great work before them.

clean passed over, that the ark of the LORD passed over, and the priests in the presence of the people.

12 And the children of Reuben, and the children of Gad, and half the tribe of Manasseh, passed over armed before the children of Israel, as Moses spake unto them:

13 About forty thousand prepared for war, passed over before the LORD unto battle, to the plains of Jericho.

14 ¶ On that day the LORD magnified Joshua in the sight of all Israel, and they feared him as they feared Moses, all the days of his life.

15 And the LORD spake unto Joshua, saying,

16 Command the priests that bear the ark of the testimony, that they come up out of Jordan.

17 Joshua therefore commanded the priests, saying, Come ye up out of Jordan.

VER. 12, 13. Parenthetic verses. (See notes on chap. i. 13, 14.)

Prepared for war. Rather, "selected troops." (Comp. vi. 7.)

VER. 14. See on chap. iii. 7.

VER. 15-17. A special signal, such as we supposed at ver. 2, is given by God for Joshua to command the end of the miracle by the exit of the ark from the river's bed. It is not necessary to suppose a new appearance of God, or a vision, on each occasion when the phrase is used, "the Lord spake unto Joshua."

VER. 16. *Ark of the testimony.* In chap. iii. 3, 11, 17, iv. 7, 18, the ark is called *the ark of the covenant of Jehovah*, or *the ark of the covenant of the Lord (Adon)*. In chap. iii. 6, 8, 14, iv. 9, it is called simply *the ark of the covenant.* In chap. iii. 13, iv. 5, 11, it is called simply *the ark of Jehovah.* Here it is called *the ark of the testi-*

18 And it came to pass, when the priests that bare the ark of the covenant of the LORD were come up out of the midst of Jordan, *and* the soles of the priests' feet were lifted up unto the dry land, that the waters of Jordan returned unto their place, and flowed over all his banks, as *they did* before.

mony. In Exodus, Leviticus, and Numbers, it is generally styled " the ark of the *testimony.*" It is the name first given to it (see Ex. xxv. 16, 21, 22), as containing the " testimony," or " two tables of testimony" (Ex. xxxi. 18), written with the finger of God. In Deuteronomy, the usage appears to call it " the ark of the *covenant,*" as carrying the testimony on which God's covenant with his people was based. This covenant was with God, as against any covenant with the Canaanites. (See Ex. xxxiv. 10–15, and compare with ver. 27–29 of the same chapter.) In Deuteronomy, when Moses addresses the people on approaching Canaan, it is natural to emphasize the *covenant,* and this is followed in Joshua. Only in this instance in Joshua is the ark called by its old title of "ark of the testimony." The ark was, as it were, the holy chest containing Israel's title-deed to Canaan, with the conditions annexed. It was the *testimony* of a *covenant* with God. (Comp. Josh. i. 7, 8.)

VER. 18. *Lifted up.* The word is translated " rooted out," in Job xviii. 14. It means, " to be torn or dragged away with difficulty," and here refers to the drawing of the feet out of the muddy bottom and sides of the river-bed. The river-bed

19 ¶ And the people came up out of Jordan on the tenth *day* of the first month, and encamped in Gilgal, in the east border of Jericho.

20 And those twelve stones which they took out of Jordan, did Joshua pitch in Gilgal.

21 And he spake unto the children of Israel, saying, When your children shall ask their fathers in time to come, saying, What *mean* these stones?

22 Then ye shall let your children know, saying, Israel came over this Jordan on dry land.

23 For the LORD your God dried up the waters of Jordan from before you, until ye were passed over, as the LORD your God did to the Red sea, which he dried up from before us, until we were gone over:

24 That all the people of the earth might know the hand of the LORD, that it *is* mighty: that ye might fear the LORD your God for ever.

had been made dry, only so far as that no running water flowed through it, but God had not carried the miracle so far as to turn the mud into arid soil. The " economy of miracles," as it is called, is to be seen in this.

VER. 19. *Tenth day.* The day for setting apart the paschal lamb (Ex. xii. 3).

Gilgal. See note on ver. 8.

In the east border of Jericho, i.e., at the eastern edge of the territory under the sway of the King of Jericho. This would lead us to suppose that Gilgal was very near the Jordan.

VER. 20–24. See note on ver. 7.

Pitch. Rather, " set up."

VER. 24. God intended that the miraculous cross- ing of the Jordan should show the *people of the land* that Jehovah (and not men) was dealing with them, and should beget in *Israel* a deep reverence for their God, and a fear of disobeying his will.

CHAPTER V.

1 AND it came to pass, when all the kings of the Amorites which *were* on the side of Jordan westward, and all the kÏngs of the Canaanites, which *were* by the sea, heard that the LORD had dried up the waters of Jordan from before the children of Israel, until we were passed over, that their heart melted; neither was there spirit in them any more, because of the children of Israel.

VER. 1. *Amorites.* The Amorites were probably the largest Canaanitish tribe in this portion of the lands of the children of Canaan, as the Hittites were the largest in the region of Lebanon and the Euphrates. Hence they are here spoken of as representing in general the tribes in the mountain-region. The name " *Canaanites* " is also used here in like manner for all the tribes along the Mediterranean Sea, on the low plains. The other four tribes — the Hivites, Perizzites, Girgashites, and Jebusites — were of inferior importance ; and the Hittites in Palestine proper were but few in number. It will be remembered that Sihon's kingdom on the east of Jordan, conquered by Israel, was an Amoritish kingdom (Num. xxi. 21–31.)

Melted. As in chap. ii. 11.

Spirit. Lit., "breath." The melting of the heart and the stopping of the breath are most strong and natural expressions for utter despair.

3   D

V. Preparations for the Conquest.   (Ver. 2 to
chap. vii.)

1. *Circumcision and Passover.*

2 ¶ At that time the Lord said unto Joshua, Make
thee sharp knives, and circumcise again the children of
Israel the second time.

Ver. 2. The Lord's words here, and in ver. 9,
may have been given to Joshua at one revelation
after crossing the Jordan, the words in ver. 9
being proleptic.

Sharp knives. In Ps. lxxxix. 43, "tsur cherev"
means "edge of the sword." Hence our trans-
lators have translated the phrase here "charvoth
tsurim," "swords of edges," or "sharp knives."
But it is better, with our margin, to take "tsurim" in its ordinary meaning of "stone" or "rock,"
and translate the words by "knives of stone." So
the Septuagint has it. And in Herodotus (ii. 86),
we see that the ancients used stone knives for such
purposes. (Comp. Ex. iv. 25.)

*Circumcise again the children of Israel the sec-
ond time.* They were all circumcised who came
out of Egypt, but there had been no circumcis-
ing since. The "second time" only means that
once they had been a circumcised people. It does
not mean that this was a second general circumcision. For this Hebrew use of the phrase, "second time," see Isa. xi. 11, where it refers to the
first recovery of a people *once before* in their own
land.

3 And Joshua made him sharp knives, and circumcised the children of Israel at the hill of the foreskins.

4 And this *is* the cause why Joshua did circumcise: All the people that came out of Egypt, *that were* males, *even* all the men of war died in the wilderness by the way, after they came out of Egypt.

5 Now all the people that came out were circumcised; but all the people *that were* born in the wilderness by the way as they came forth out of Egypt, *them* they had not circumcised.

6 For the children of Israel walked forty years in the wilderness, till all the people *that were* men of war which came out of Egypt were consumed, because they obeyed not the voice of the LORD: unto whom the LORD sware that he would not shew them the land which the LORD sware unto their fathers that he would give us, a land that floweth with milk and honey.

7 And their children, *whom* he raised up in their stead, them Joshua circumcised: for they were uncircumcised, because they had not circumcised them by the way.

VER. 3. *Hill of the foreskins.* Heb., "Gibrah haaraloth." Identical with Gilgal, as we see by ver. 9.

VER. 4–7. The *fact* is stated here, that no child was circumcised in the desert, but the *reason* is not stated. Some deny the fact, and say the word " all " in ver. 5 must not be pressed, that it was only *all who were born after the sinful unbelief and rebellion*, for which God made them dwell thirty-eight years longer in the desert, and hence that the lack of circumcision was part of the frown of God. But this seems very forced. We should have expected some allusion to it in the narrative, had this been the case. We, therefore, take the fact literally, and consider the ordinary reason supposed a good one, that the unsettled style of life

> 8 And it came to pass when they had done circum-
> cising all the people, that they abode in their places in
> the camp, till they were whole.
>
> 9 And the LORD said unto Joshua, This day have
> I rolled away the reproach of Egypt from off you :
> Wherefore the name of the place is called Gilgal unto
> this day.
>
> 10 ¶ And the children of Israel encamped in Gilgal,
> and kept the passover on the fourteenth day of the
> month at even, in the plains of Jericho.

in the desert exempted them, by some special permission of God not recorded.

VER. 8. *All the people, i.e.,* who needed circumcision.   Those men who had left Egypt under
twenty years of age, and who were now over forty,
had been circumcised in Egypt.   And we may estimate these at three hundred thousand, an ample
force to defend the camp while the rest were dis-
abled, and to perform the rite.   So there was no
remarkable exposure to the enemy, as many have
supposed.

VER. 9. *The reproach of Egypt.*   That is, the
reproach which Egypt cast upon Israel (as in Ex.
xiv. 3), that they were entrapped in the desert.
(Comp. Ex. xxxii. 12; Num. xiv. 13; Deut. ix. 28;
also Zeph. ii. 8.)   The reproach was rolled away by
their entry upon the promised land and celebrating
the covenant, now fulfilled in its first instalment,
by the adoption of its mark.

VER. 10. *On the fourteenth day of the month.*
Three days after the circumcision, the passover is
kept, a second solemn acknowledgment and con-
firmation of the covenant, whose glorious issues
they were now beginning to enjoy.

11 And they did eat of the old corn of the land on the morrow after the passover, unleavened cakes and parched *corn* in the self-same day.

12 ¶ And the manna ceased on the morrow after they had eaten of the old corn of the land; neither had the children of Israel manna any more; but they did eat of the fruit of the land of Canaan that year.

13 ¶ And it came to pass when Joshua was by Jericho, that he lifted up his eyes and looked, and behold, there stood a man over against him with his sword drawn in his hand: and Joshua went unto him, and said unto him, *Art* thou for us, or for our adversaries?

VER. 11. The country in which they encamped at Gilgal is arid and barren. So it is not till they had been there five days that they obtained some of the *produce* of the land, perhaps by a foraging raid.

Old corn. Rather, "produce." So in the next verse.

VER. 12. The manna ceases on the sixteenth of Nisan, and now the provision prepared on the east of Jordan stands them in good part, until they can obtain a full supply from their new land. (See note on chap. i. 11.)

2. *The Special Appearance of God.*

VER. 13. *Was by Jericho.* The occasion of this vision must have been a time of retirement on the part of Joshua, and very probably a time of prayer. The place may have been near Gilgal, as the headquarters of Israel seem to have continued at Gilgal during all the remarkable siege of Jericho. "Near Gilgal" would be equivalent to "by Jericho." A warrior suddenly appears before Joshua. Israel's hero instantly challenges him. The doubting char-

> 14 And he said, Nay; but *as* captain of the host of
> the LORD am I now come. And Joshua fell on his
> face to the earth, and did worship, and said unto him,
> What saith my lord unto his servant?
> 15 And the captain of the LORD's host said unto
> Joshua, Loose thy shoe from off thy foot, for the place
> whereon thou standest *is* holy: and Joshua did so.

acter of his question suggests the notion that it
was in the night-time, and that therefore Joshua
could not readily discern whether it was an Isra-
elite or not.

VER. 14. Lit., *Nay, but I, prince of the host of
Jehovah, have now come.* " Prince of the host of
Jehovah " would be understood by Joshua to be a
ruler of angels. And therefore he immediately
offers him obeisance. The worship is only such
worship as one created being might offer another.
He calls him " my lord," which is not the title (in
the Hebrew) he would have used if he had supposed the angel to be the Divine Angel, coequal
with God.

VER. 15. *Loose thy shoe,* &c. Now the command
of the angel, the pronouncing of the ground holy
where such an interview was held, and the likeness
in all this to the interview of God with Moses at
the bush, must have convinced Joshua that this
was indeed God himself, and not the person of a
created angel, that stood before him.

CHAPTER VI.

1 Now Jericho was straitly shut up, because of the children of Israel: none went out, and none came in.

2 And the LORD said unto Joshua, See, I have given into thine hand Jericho, and the king thereof, *and* the mighty men of valour.

VER. 1. Merely parenthetical.

VER. 2. *The Lord.* Lit., " Jehovah," the same as *the prince of the host of the Lord,* in chap. v. 15. It is Jehovah-Jesus, the Lord of angels, " the brightness of the Father's glory, the express image of his person " (Heb. i. 3). He appears as a warrior, because he wishes to impress upon Joshua that he, the Lord, is fighting with Israel against Canaan. It is not Israel's war, but God's war, against a depraved and God-defiant people. (Compare the appearance of our Lord as against sinners, represented in Rev. xix. 11–16.)

VER. 2. *I have given.* Notice how often God repeats the thought to Israel that all their action against Canaan was as his agents, and not at all as of themselves. Vengeance or cruelty in their conquest had no more place necessarily than the same qualities are necessarily found in a sheriff who executes a capital sentence.

3 And ye shall compass the city, all *ye* men of war, *and* go round about the city once: thus shalt thou do six days.

4 And seven priests shall bear before the ark seven trumpets of rams' horns: and the seventh day ye shall compass the city seven times, and the priests shall blow with the trumpets.

5 And it shall come to pass, that when they make a long *blast* with the ram's horn, *and* when ye hear the sound of the trumpet, all the people shall shout with a great shout: and the wall of the city shall fall down flat, and the people shall ascend up every man straight before him.

VER. 3–5. Once a day for six days the entire force of armed men, perhaps six hundred thousand men, was to march around the city, and with them seven * priests, bearing each a horn and blowing upon it, preceding the ark. On the seventh day the procession should march seven times around the devoted city, and then a long blast from the horns should be accompanied by a shout from the whole army, when the walls should sink upon themselves, and the army should march directly into the city, every man in a straight course from his standing-place.

VER. 4. *Trumpets of rams' horns.* More truly, "shrill clarions." The word translated "trumpets" means a horn, as we see by ver. 5, where

---

* The number "seven," used here in the enumeration of priests, trumpets, days, and circuits, *must* have a special significance. Some consider it a combination of four (the earth's number) and three (the divine number), and thus representing God's reconciling peace, *i.e.*, the number of redemption. Some think that here is a reference to the seven great days of the world's history and the final judgment.

6 ¶ And Joshua the son of Nun called the priests, and said unto them, Take up the ark of the covenant, and let seven priests bear seven trumpets of rams' horns before the ark of the LORD.

7 And he said unto the people, Pass on, and compass the city, and let him that is armed pass on before the ark of the LORD.

8 ¶ And it came to pass, when Joshua had spoken unto the people, that the seven priests bearing the seven trumpets of rams' horns passed on before the LORD, and blew with the trumpets: and the ark of the covenant of the LORD followed them.

9 ¶ And the armed men went before the priests that blew with the trumpets, and the rere-ward came after the ark, *the priests* going on, and blowing with the trumpets.

the Hebrew word "horn" is used. It was a horn that produced a loud, clear sound. The word translated "rams' horn" is the familiar word "jubilee," and refers originally to an exciting shrill clangor. Trumpet-sounds were tokens of the divine presence and power (Ex. xix. 16).

3. *The Fall of Jericho.*

VER. 7. *Him that is armed.* Rather, "the selected troops." (See on chap. iv. 13.)

VER. 8. *Before the Lord.* That is, "before the ark of the Lord." The ark was God's representative, as the pillar of cloud had been previously.

VER. 9. The *chalutz*, or "selected troops," went before the ark; and the *measseph*, or "massed troops," followed the ark. This special arrangement is omitted in the record of the Lord's command in ver. 2–5, where for brevity's sake the orders are only generally stated.

3*

10 And Joshua had commanded the people, saying, Ye shall not shout, nor make any noise with your voice, neither shall *any* word proceed out of your mouth, until the day I bid you shout, then shall ye shout.

11 So the ark of the LORD compassed the city, going about *it* once: and they came into the camp, and lodged in the camp.

12 ¶ And Joshua rose early in the morning, and the priests took up the ark of the LORD.

13 And seven priests bearing seven trumpets of rams' horns before the ark of the LORD went on continually, and blew with the trumpets: and the armed men went before them; but the rere-ward came after the ark of the LORD, *the priests* going on, and blowing with the trumpets.

14 And the second day they compassed the city once, and returned into the camp. So they did six days.

15 And it came to pass on the seventh day, that they rose early about the dawning of the day, and compassed the city after the same manner seven times: only on that day they compassed the city seven times.

16 And it came to pass at the seventh time, when the priests blew with the trumpets, Joshua said unto the people, Shout; for the LORD hath given you the city.

17 ¶ And the city shall be accursed, *even* it, and all that *are* therein, to the LORD: only Rahab the harlot shall live, she and all that *are* with her in the house, because she hid the messengers that we sent.

VER. 10. In perfect silence the march was to continue, till the last circuit of the last day (ver. 16).

VER. 11. *The camp*, *i.e.*, at Gilgal.

VER. 13. See on verses 4 and 9.

VER. 15. *Early*. To give time for the seven circuits.

VER. 17–19. These also are special directions, not recorded in ver. 2–5. (Comp. on ver. 9.)

Accursed. Heb. " cherem." In Lev. xxvii. 28,

18 And ye, in any wise keep *yourselves* from the accursed thing, lest ye make *yourselves* accursed, when ye take of the accursed thing, and make the camp of Israel a curse, and trouble it.

19 But all the silver, and gold, and vessels of brass and iron, *are* consecrated unto the Lord: they shall come into the treasury of the Lord.

20 So the people shouted when *the priests* blew with the trumpets: and it came to pass, when the people heard the sound of the trumpet, and the people shouted with a great shout, that the wall fell down flat, so that the people went up into the city, every man straight before him, and they took the city.

is the law of " cherem," or the *devoted* thing. It implied an entire separation to the Lord : if of material property, by consecration to his service ; and if of persons, to death. Hence here, *Rahab shall live*, is antithetic to the general " cherem."

Ver. 18. " Only do ye beware of the *cherem*, lest ye make *cherem*, and take of the *cherem*, and put the camp of Israel to *cherem*." The last two clauses are an enlargement of the first two ; thus, " Beware of the *cherem*, so as not to take of the *cherem*, lest ye make *cherem*, by putting the camp of Israel to *cherem*." (Comp. Deut. vii. 25, 26.)

Ver. 19. *Consecrated.* Lit., " holiness."

Ver. 20. The directions are followed. The priests make the long blast (yet only the word for the ordinary blowing is used here), the host hear and respond with a mighty shout, the walls fall in upon themselves, as if shaken by an earthquake, and the host march in, each man in a straight line from his standing-place.

21 And they utterly destroyed all that *was* in the
city, both man and woman, young and old, and ox, and
sheep, and ass, with the edge of the sword.

VER. 21. The *cherem*, so far as the persons in
Jericho were concerned, was literally observed. It
is a favorite objection to the morality of the Old
Testament Scriptures, and hence to its teachings
regarding God, that Israel thus slew men, women,
and children in their conquest of Canaan. We
have already called attention to God's constant use
of Israel as his agent in this whole matter. He
who would not be counted cruel in sending the
pestilence and destroying a people, ought not to be
charged with cruelty when he uses human agency
in the same manner. So that the God of the Old
Testament cannot be called a cruel God any more
than the God of nature can be so accused. Such a
teaching, therefore, regarding God is nothing
against the Old Testament, or against the course
of Israel as God's people. God's ways are above
us. We cannot know his motives or his purposes.
We must acknowledge his wisdom, and be still,
knowing that he is God. He has revealed himself as Love, and yet we know that he permits
and ordains ruin and disaster among the children
of men. But the Judge of all the earth does
justly. In all this matter of Israel's conquest of
Canaan, we must keep ever before us the mere
agency of Israel throughout. The divine order
permeates all they do. So there is *no example
here for men, without orders from God direct*. The

22 But Joshua had said unto the two men that had spied out the country, Go into the harlot's house, and bring out thence the woman, and all that she hath, as ye sware unto her.

23 And the young men that were spies went in, and · brought out Rahab, and her father, and her mother, and her brethren, and all that she had; and they brought out all her kindred, and left them without the camp of Israel.

24 And they burnt the city with fire, and all that *was* therein: only the silver, and the gold, and the vessels of brass and of iron, they put into the treasury of the house of the LORD.

25 And Joshua saved Rahab the harlot alive, and her father's household, and all that she had; and she dwelleth in Israel *even* unto this day; because she hid the messengers which Joshua sent to spy out Jericho.

26 ¶ And Joshua abjured *them* at that time, saying, Cursed *be* the man before the LORD, that riseth up and buildeth this city Jericho; he shall lay the foundation thereof in his first-born, and in his youngest *son* shall he set up the gates of it.

case is unique, and cannot constitute a precedent. (See Appendix.)

VER. 22. *All that she hath.* Like the "all that they have" of chap. ii. 13, this refers only to human beings, not to goods. It is explained in the next verse as "all her kindred," or, literally, "all her families;" *i.e.*, all the households belonging to her father's stock.

VER. 23. *Without the camp.* They could not enter until they had been ritually prepared as proselytes.

VER. 25. *Even unto this day.* (See on chap. iv. 9.)

VER. 26. The ruined site was to be a witness to succeeding generations of God's favor to his people,

27 So the LORD was with Joshua; and his fame was
noised throughout all the country.

and of his judgment upon sin. Jericho was given
to Benjamin (chap. xviii. 21), and people dwelt
there after this, before Hiel rebuilt it, as we see by
Judg. i. 16, and iii. 13, as compared with Deut.
xxxiv. 3. It was simply an unfortified, open town
or straggling village ; and hence the Kenites, who
would not dwell in fortified towns, were willing to
abide there for a time (Judg. i. 16. Comp. Judg.
iv. 11; 1 Chron. ii. 55; Jer. xxxv. 7, 10). The
curse of Joshua was against any one who should
rebuild Jericho as a fortification. Hence he speaks
of " foundation " and " gates."

In his first born ; in his youngest son. " In " is
used in Hebrew for " at the price or pay of." Thus,
in Gen. xxix. 18, Jacob says, " I will serve thee
seven years *in* Rachel thy younger daughter ; "
that is, at the pay of Rachel. So here, " at the
cost of his first-born." It is not said that all the
man's children should die during the rebuilding,
but it seems to be implied. Hiel, of Bethel, more
than five hundred years afterward, dared the
curse, and was punished accordingly (1 Kings
xvi. 34).

VER. 27. By the crossing of Jordan and the
taking of Jericho, under grand miraculous exhibi-
tions of God's presence and guidance, Joshua's
position as Israel's great captain was confirmed
and his name feared by the people of Canaan.

CHAPTER VII.

VI. The Conquest. (Chap. vii.-xii.)

1 But the children of Israel committed a trespass in the accursed thing: for Achan, the son of Carmi, the son of Zabdi, the son of Zerah, of the tribe of Judah, took of the accursed thing: and the anger of the Lord was kindled against the children of Israel.

Thus far Israel had not gained aught by military prowess. Miraculous intervention had secured the crossing of the Jordan and the capture of Jericho. But now the conquest by their own arm (under God) was to begin. They had been vividly taught by the events of the preceding month to be *trustful* before God, and this necessary lesson having been given, they were now to go forward and conquer the land for the Lord who sent them. But their conduct was very soon to show that a new teaching of God's severity against *disobedience* was necessary. They were to learn that their trust in God against their enemies was to be proportioned to their own obedience to God.

1. *The Repulse before Ai.*

Ver. 1. *The children of Israel committed a trespass.* The whole nation is so connected with each family within it, that the sin of one family mars the progress of all. If one member suffer, all suffer

> 2 And Joshua sent men from Jericho to Ai, which
> *is* beside Beth-aven, on the east side of Beth-el, and
> spake unto them, saying, Go up and view the country.
> And the men went up and viewed Ai.

with it (Rom. xii. 26). God treats his people as
one, because they *are* one. Nature testifies to the
oneness of the race. Grace uses this nature in the
constitution of the redeemed family of God.

Committed a trespass. Lit., " deceived a deceit."
Achan practised a deceit with regard to the *cherem.*

Achan. He stands forth in sad conspicuity in
the record in 1 Chron. ii. 7. He was fourth in
descent from Judah, according to this list; but as
many names were left out of Jewish lists (names
of unimportant men or of those who died quite
early in life), we cannot be sure that there were
only four generations between Achan and Judah.
It was a member of the leading tribe (in point of
size and birthright precedence) who first marred
the symmetry and success of Israel conquest.

The anger of the Lord is his holiness outburn-
ing against unrighteousness. See Ex. iv. 14, where
the phrase is used toward Moses, the friend of God
(Ex. xxxiii. 11). In these anthropomorphic repre-
sentations of God, we must divest the affections of
all the sinful qualities they have in man.

VER. 2. A reconnoitring party are sent to examine Ai, as the next important city to conquer
on Israel's way to the very centre of the land,
where they were to enter anew into solemn covenant with God. The host still encamp at Gilgal,
stretching out over the plain to Jericho. *Ai* is

3 And they returned to Joshua, and said unto him, Let not all the people go up; but let about two or three thousand men go up and smite Ai: *and* make not all the people to labour thither; for they *are but* few.

here mentioned as beside or near Bethaven, and east of Bethel. In 1 Sam. xiii. 5, Michmash is said to be east of Bethaven. In Hos. x. 5, the idol-calves of Bethel are called by a paronomasia the calves of Bethaven, which would indicate that Bethel and Bethaven were near together. Now the sites of Bethel and Michmash are identified beyond a doubt, Michmash being five miles south and east of Bethel, its longitude being less than three miles east of that of Bethel. Both Ai and Bethaven must lie somewhere between these two points, so that Michmash may be eastward of Bethaven, and Ai, which is near Bethaven, be eastward of Bethel. Van der Velde's identification of Ai with Tell el-Hajar, and of Bethaven with the ruins on the rocky height about a mile southeast of Bethel, and about a mile west of Ai, is undoubtedly correct. Tell el-Hajar is on the southern brow of the deep Wady el-Mutyah, and shows no other remains of antiquity than a broken cistern. The distance of Ai from Jericho is thirteen miles, and the route is along the base of Kuruntul, and then directly westward up the deep Wady el-Mutyah. This wady forms a natural road into the heart of the country.

VER. 3. The spies return, come back from Ai, and advise that only a small band of two thousand or three thousand be sent against the city. They

E

4 So there went up thither of the people about three
thousand men: and they fled before the men of Ai.
5 And the men of Ai smote of them about thirty and
six men: for they chased them *from* before the gate
even unto Shebarim, and smote them in the going
down. wherefore the hearts of the people melted, and
became as water.
6 ¶ And Joshua rent his clothes, and fell to the
earth upon his face before the ark of the LORD until
the even-tide, he and the elders of Israel, and put dust
upon their heads.

were, doubtless, full of what God had done at
Jericho, with which Ai was a very small city in
comparison, and it may have been a commendable
faith which prompted their report. Ai had but
twelve thousand inhabitants in all (chap. viii. 25),
and hence may not have had over three thousand
fighting men.

VER. 4. The little detachment probably pro-
ceeded up the Mutyah directly to the city gate,
using no stratagem whatever.

VER. 5. *About thirty and six men.* Why
"about"? Perhaps some dangerously wounded
were counted in the number.

Unto Shebarim. Or, by translation, *to the broken
places*, *i.e.*, to the steep broken sides of the Mutyah.

And smote them in the going down, *i.e.*, along the
descent of the great wady toward Jericho.

Melted. (See on chap. ii. 9, 11.) The people
had trusted their success rather than God. So
when success ends, they faint.

VER. 6. Joshua and the representative council
of the Israelitish nation assume the attitude and
condition of deepest grief and abasement before

7 And Joshua said, Alas! O Lord GOD, wherefore hast thou at all brought this people over Jordan, to deliver us into the hand of the Amorites, to destroy us? would to God we had been content, and dwelt on the other side Jordan!

8 O Lord, what shall I say, when Israel turneth their backs before their enemies!

9 For the Canaanites, and all the inhabitants of the land shall hear *of it,* and shall environ us round, and cut off our name from the earth: and what wilt thou do unto thy great name?

the ark until the time of evening sacrifice. It would appear from this passage and from chap. viii. 33, that the tabernacle was not yet set up in the new land, but awaited the arrival at its permanent position. In this case the ark would be exposed to view. The parts of the ritual that would require the erection of the tabernacle were, doubtless, suspended.

VER. 7–9. There is a strange mingling of unbelief and of zeal for God in Joshua's cry. He suggests that God has intended to destroy his people, and wishes they had remained in the conquered countries east of Jordan. He expects, also, saddest results from the defeat. But with all this, he shows a deep concern for the honor of God's name, which he fears has been compromised. The greatest of saints break down under trial, and show how weak they are. God mercifully remembers they are dust, and bears with them tenderly.

VER. 7. *Would to God.* The name of God does not appear in the Hebrew. It is simply " would that."

10 ¶ And the Lord said unto Joshua, Get thee up; wherefore liest thou thus upon thy face?

11 Israel hath sinned, and they have also transgressed my covenant which I commanded them: for they have even taken of the accursed thing, and have also stolen, and dissembled also, and they have put *it* even among their own stuff.

12 Therefore the children of Israel could not stand before their enemies, *but* turned *their* backs before their enemies, because they were accursed: neither will I be with you any more, except ye destroy the accursed from among you.

2. *Achan's Sin and Punishment.*

VER. 10. The Lord's speech to Joshua at this time must have been in the presence of the elders. We may, therefore, suppose that it came through Urim and Thummim, and by the voice of Eleazar the high-priest. The rebuke in the words of the Lord is a strong one. The question is sharp.

VER. 11. Israel had both sinned in the theft and deceit of Achan, and had broken the covenant so solemnly made at Sinai and remembered at Gilgal. They had taken of the *cherem*, they had stolen, they had deceived, they had made the *cherem* private property. In the Hebrew, the six allegations are connected together by the particle " gam " (also), five times repeated, giving great solemnity to the charge.

VER. 12. *They were accursed.* Lit., " they were for *cherem*." They had identified themselves with *cherem*, and so must suffer, so long as this identification should continue, for all that is *cherem* must be destroyed.

13 Up, sanctify the people, and say, Sanctify yourselves against to-morrow: for thus saith the LORD God of Israel, *There is* an accursed thing in the midst of thee, O Israel: thou canst not stand before thine enemies, until ye take away the accursed thing from among you.

14 In the morning therefore ye shall be brought according to your tribes: and it shall be, *that* the tribe which the LORD taketh shall come according to the families *thereof:* and the family which the LORD shall take shall come by households ; and the household which the LORD shall take shall come man by man.

15 And it shall be, *that* he that is taken with the accursed thing shall be burnt with fire, he and all that he hath : because he hath transgressed the covenant of the LORD, and because he hath wrought folly in Israel.

VER. 13. *Up, sanctify the people.* " Up " from the bowed attitude of humiliation and grief. For the sanctification, see on chap. iii. 5.

VER. 14. On the morrow would be the search for the offenders. That very evening they would make their solemn ritual preparation for the investigation. The fearful nature of sin is shown most forcibly in this memorable scene. How can man make light of that which God thus stamps with his holy indignation and righteous judgments?

VER. 15. The burning with fire was the most striking token of the consuming wrath of a holy God. (See Heb. xii. 29, as comp. with Heb. x. 27.)

All that he hath. All his family. (See on chap. vi. 22. See also ver. 25.) The family had, no doubt, been cognizant of Achan's crime, and had not revealed it, for in Deut. xxiv. 16, it is expressly declared by God that the children shall not be put to death for the fathers.

16 ¶ So Joshua rose up early in the morning, and brought Israel by their tribes; and the tribe of Judah was taken:

17 And he brought the family of Judah; and he took the family of the Zarhites : and he brought the family of the Zarhites man by man: and Zabdi was taken:

18 And he brought his household man by man; and Achan the son of Carmi, the son of Zabdi, the son of Zerah, of the tribe of Judah, was taken.

Folly. The word is used for a great wickedness. For the two elements of the crime see on ver. 11.

VER. 16. *Joshua rose up early.* Joshua, of course, arose from his prostrate position before the ark, and that evening sanctified the people. But no mention is made of this, as it was unnecessary. But the narrative passes over at once to the next day and its investigation.

VER. 16–18. The process here described was wrought, we may suppose, through the use of the Urim and Thummim (see Num. xxvii. 21), of which we know almost nothing in detail. The lot may have been used also.

Zarhites, *i.e.,* the branch of the tribe of Judah, called from their ancestor, Zerah, the son of Judah. The tribe in Heb. is *shévet* ("rod" or "stem"), and the family is *mishpachah* ("spreading"), but in ver. 17 the *tribe* of Judah is called the *family* of Judah, for, after all, the words are comparative words. Next to the *family* was the house, or *bayith,* and then the individual man, or *gever.*

Zabdi was, perhaps, the oldest of Achan's an-

19 And Joshua said unto Achan, My son, give, I
pray thee, glory to the LORD God of Israel, and make
confession unto him; and tell me now what thou hast
done, hide *it* not from me.

20 And Achan answered Joshua, and said, Indeed I
have sinned against the LORD God of Israel, and thus
and thus have I done.

21 When I saw among the spoils a goodly Babylonish garment, and two hundred shekels of silver, and
a wedge of gold of fifty shekels weight, then I coveted
them, and took them, and behold, they *are* hid in the
earth in the midst of my tent, and the silver under it.

cestors then living, his grandfather, and thus the
head of the *bayith*, or house. Between Zerah and
Zabdi, in this case, there must have been several
generations omitted in the genealogy. (See on
ver. 1.)

VER. 19. *My son.* Joshua is tender, even when
acting as a judge and executioner.

Give glory to the Lord. (Comp. John ix. 14.)
A solemn form of adjuring an accursed man to
confess. Confession is anticipating the discovery
God will make of the crime, and thus is a tribute
to his omniscience.

VER. 21. *Babylonish garment.* Heb., *addereth
shinar.* The *addereth* was a large outer cloak.
The Babylonish or Shinar goods were well known
in ancient times throughout the East for their fine
texture and rich embroidery. The figures of men
and beasts, which some suppose were worked on such
a garment, would of themselves make the article a
forbidden one to a Jew. The Babylonian textures
are spoken of by Arrian (vi. 29). The figure of
a Babylonish king, of a period three hundred years

22 ¶ So Joshua sent messengers, and they ran unto
the tent, and behold, *it was* hid in his tent, and the
silver under it.

23 And they took them out of the midst of the tent,
and brought them unto Joshua, and unto all the children of Israel, and laid them out before the LORD.

24 And Joshua, and all Israel with him, took Achan
the son of Zerah, and the silver, and the garment, and
the wedge of gold, and his sons, and his daughters,
and his oxen, and his asses, and his sheep, and his
tent, and all that he had : and they brought them
unto the valley of Achor.

later than Achan, engraved on a large black stone
in the British Museum, represents him clad in a
large outer robe embroidered in a very elaborate
and delicate pattern.

Two hundred shekels of silver would equal about
one hundred and twenty dollars of silver ; of course
at that day worth probably twenty times what it is
worth to-day.

Wedge of gold. Lit., " tongue of gold." This
gold ornament of fifty shekels weight would be
worth about two hundred and twenty dollars.

The silver under it. That is, the tongue of gold
was wrapped up in the Babylonish garment, and
placed over the more bulky silver.

VER. 23. *Laid them out before the Lord.* Lit.,
" poured them out before Jehovah," *i.e.*, poured
them out of the cloth in which they carried them
from the hiding-place. " Before Jehovah," is (as
at chap. vi. 8) " before the ark."

VER. 24. Achan's whole family (as guilty with
him) and all his possessions are brought to the
Valley of Achor. The valley received the name

25 And Joshua said, Why hast thou troubled us? the LORD shall trouble thee this day. And all Israel stoned him with stones, and burned them with fire, after they had stoned them with stones.

from this scene (ver. 26). Achor means "troubling," and refers to the trouble given Israel by the taking of the *cherem*. (See chap. vi. 18.) There is also a paronomasia on Achan's name. Indeed, in 1 Chron. ii. 7, Achan is called *Achar*, or "troubler." Twice the prophets refer to this valley (Isa. lxv. 10, and Hos. ii. 15), in each case using it as a token of a spiritual trouble, out of which God, through his judgments and their repentance and renewed obedience, would lead his people.

Brought them into the valley of Achor. The Heb. is, "brought them *up* to the valley of Achor." Hence (and also from the position of the valley in the description of Judah's boundary in chap. xv. 7) we must look for Achor up from the Jericho plain. It was probably that portion of Wady Kelt where its upward course enters the mountains, and where now is the ruined castle of Kakon. It is less than two miles from Jericho.

VER. 25. *Why hast thou* TROUBLED *us? the Lord shall* TROUBLE *thee.* There is here, as in the *lex talionis* (Ex. xxi. 23–25), an allusion to that perfect justice which underlies the whole of the divine administration. The atonement of Jesus Christ meets this in behalf of the believing sinner.

Stoned him; burned them. Achan is made prominent in the first expression, as the leader in the crime.

4

26 And they raised over him a great heap of stones unto this day. So the LORD turned from the fierceness of his anger: wherefore the name of that place was called, The valley of Achor, unto this day.

VER. 26. *A great heap of stones unto this day.* That is, probably, not only a heap remaining to this day, but which is constantly increased by the passers by throwing stones upon the pile in their indignation against the crime of Achan. On the way to Sinai from Egypt, the traveller passes such a cairn, called "Husan Abu Zenneh," which is kicked by every Arab as he goes by, and which, I believe, is increased in that manner, and for a like reason.

So the Lord turned from the fierceness of his anger. Such passages as these need to be carefully considered, as impressing the mind with the fearful character of sin and its certainty of punishment, before the holiness of God can be vindicated. This whole department of revealed truth, which is the only true basis of Christian doctrine and Christian life, is more and more ignored by the naturalism of the day.

CHAPTER VIII.

1 AND the LORD said unto Joshua, Fear not, neither be thou dismayed: take all the people of war with thee, and arise, go up to Ai: see, I have given into thy hand the king of Ai, and his people, and his city, and his land:
2 And thou shalt do to Ai and her king, as thou didst unto Jericho and her king: only the spoil thereof, and the cattle thereof, shall ye take for a prey unto yourselves: lay thee an ambush for the city behind it.

3. *The taking of Ai.*

VER. 1. The Lord (perhaps through the high-priest) repeats the words which gave courage to Joshua at the beginning of his administration (chap. i. 9). He needed the comforting exhortation after the bitter experiences he had just passed through. (Comp. Acts xviii. 9, 10, xxvii. 23, 24.)

Take all the people of war. God would have the entire armed host witness how completely the sin had been expiated and Israel now again counted pure before him. So all the armed men (perhaps only a section of the six hundred thousand would act as warriors at any one time) were to march up to the front of Ai and take part in its destruction.

VER. 2. *Only the spoil thereof*, &c. The *cherem* is ordered only for the human beings. The rest should be Israel's own property.

3 ¶ So Joshua arose, and all the people of war, to go up against Ai: and Joshua chose out thirty thousand mighty men of valour, and sent them away by night.

4 And he commanded them, saying, Behold, ye shall lie in wait against the city, *even* behind the city: go not very far from the city, but be ye all ready:

5 And I, and all the people that *are* with me, will approach unto the city: and it shall come to pass when they come out against us, as at the first, that we will flee before them,

6 (For they will come out after us) till we have drawn them from the city; for they will say, They flee before us, as at the first: therefore we will flee before them.

7 Then ye shall rise up from the ambush, and seize upon the city: for the LORD your God will deliver it into your hand.

8 And it shall be when ye have taken the city, *that* ye shall set the city on fire: according to the commandment of the LORD shall ye do. See, I have commanded you.

9 ¶ Joshua therefore sent them forth; and they went to lie in ambush, and abode between Beth-el and Ai, on the west side of Ai: but Joshua lodged that night among the people.

VER. 3. *Thirty thousand mighty men of valour.* These are selected, according to God's order, for an ambuscade. It was an enormous number, but God was teaching Israel at this crisis that they were to use the means they had. Perhaps in the spies' report (chap. vii. 3) and advice this idea may have been lacking. So large a body of men must seek a place of ambuscade under cover of the night. The make of the country, with its deep ravines, would help them. They were to go *behind* the city, that is, on the south-west side (*west*, according to ver. 9), as the city (if Tell el-Hajar be the site) fronted northward on the Wady el-

10 And Joshua rose up early in the morning, and numbered the people, and went up, he and the elders of Israel, before the people to Ai.

11 And all the people, *even the people* of war that *were* with him, went up, and drew nigh, and came before the city, and pitched on the north side of Ai: now *there was* a valley between them and Ai.

12 And he took about five thousand men, and set them to lie in ambush between Beth-el and Ai, on the west side of the city.

13 And when they had set the people, *even* all the host that *was* on the north of the city, and their liers in wait on the west of the city, Joshua went that night into the midst of the valley.

14 ¶ And it came to pass when the king of Ai saw *it*, that they hasted and rose up early, and the men of

Mutyah. They would naturally pass up Wady Kelt and Wady es-Suweinit to the deep hollow just west of el-Kudeirah. This would be, according to ver. 9, *between Bethel and Ai, on the west side of Ai.*

VER. 10. *Numbered the people.* Rather, " reviewed the people," *i.e.*, the people of war, the soldiery (ver. 11).

VER. 11, 12. The great host occupied the north hills of Wady el-Mutyah, in full view of the city. From this position he sent an additional five thousand to form another ambuscade at the west of the city, perhaps in one of the hollows below Burj Beitin.

VER. 13. After this display of his forces on the north hills, and this arrangement of his new ambuscade, Joshua marches down into the middle of Wady el-Mutyah, directly toward the city.

VER. 14. The people of Ai discover his position

the city went out against Israel to battle, he and all his people, at a time appointed, before the plain: but he wist not that *there were* liers in ambush against him behind the city.

15 And Joshua and all Israel made as if they were beaten before them, and fled by the way of the wilderness.

16 And all the people that *were* in Ai were called together to pursue after them: and they pursued after Joshua, and were drawn away from the city.

17 And there was not a man left in Ai, or Beth-el, that went not out after Israel: and they left the city open, and pursued after Israel.

18 And the LORD said unto Joshua, Stretch out the spear that *is* in thine hand toward Ai; for I will give it into thine hand. And Joshua stretched out the spear that *he had* in his hand toward the city.

early in the morning, and they go out to *the place of assembly* (Champ de Mars) *in front of the Arabah*, for so should be rendered the words which we have in English, "at a time appointed, before the plain." The Arabah, or "sterile plain," is the same as the wilderness of Bethaven of chap. xviii. 12, which would be the waste region at the head of Wady Mutyah.

VER. 15. *The wilderness*, *i.e.*, of Bethaven. (See preceding note.)

VER. 17. *Not a man*, *i.e.*, not a soldier. (Comp. ver. 24.) This verse shows that Bethel and Ai were very near together. If Ai were at Tell el-Hajar, the distance between the two would be less than two miles. The rout seemed to be so perfect, that the whole neighborhood joined in, thinking probably that this would be the last of Israel.

VER. 18. *The spear*. Heb., *chidhon*. Kimchi, quoted by Gesenius, says that this was a spear on

19 And the ambush arose quickly out of their place, and they ran as soon as 'he had stretched out his hand: and they entered into the city, and took it, and hasted, and set the city on fire.

20 And when the men of Ai looked behind them, they saw, and behold, the smoke of the city ascended up to heaven, and they had no power to flee this way or that way: and the people that fled to the wilderness turned back upon the pursuers.

21 And when Joshua and all Israel saw that the ambush had taken the city, and that the smoke of the city ascended, then they turned again, and slew the men of Ai.

22 And the other issued out of the city against them; so they were in the midst of Israel, some on this side, and some on that side: and they smote them, so that they let none of them remain or escape.

23 And the king of Ai they took alive, and brought him to Joshua.

which was a flag. The Lord spoke to Joshua perhaps here by the high-priest. The liers-in-wait would of course have a watch looking out for this signal, and Joshua would probably take his place on the heights at the north, whence he could easily direct every movement. They might be a mile away from Joshua, and yet clearly see this signal, if it were a red flag on the end of a spear.

VER. 20. *Power.* Heb., "hands." The people of Ai and Bethel at once saw the stratagem, and discovered that, instead of being victors, they were victims. Ability to escape, moreover, was taken away. Their "hands" were gone. The Ai people *could* not flee, and the Israelites *stopped* fleeing.

VER. 22. *Remain or escape, i.e.,* remain alive on the field or escape from it. The King of Ai is especially excepted, but even he only for a short season.

24 And it came to pass when Israel had made an end of slaying all the inhabitants of Ai in the field, in the wilderness wherein they chased them, and when they were all fallen on the edge of the sword, until they were consumed, that all the Israelites returned unto Ai, and smote it with the edge of the sword.

25 And *so* it was, *that* all that fell that day, both of men and women, *were* twelve thousand, *even* all the men of Ai.

26 For Joshua drew not his hand back wherewith he stretched out the spear, until he had utterly destroyed all the inhabitants of Ai.

27 Only the cattle and the spoil of that city Israel took for a prey unto themselves, according unto the word of the LORD which he commanded Joshua.

28 And Joshua burnt Ai, and made it an heap for ever, *even* a desolation unto this day.

29 And the king of Ai he hanged on a tree until even-tide: and as soon as the sun was down, Joshua commanded that they should take his carcass down from the tree, and cast it at the entering of the gate of the city, and raise thereon a great heap of stones, *that remaineth* unto this day.

VER. 25. *Twelve thousand.* These represented Ai, but all Bethel's warriors must have perished also, and we must count them as at least three thousand more.

VER. 26. *Drew not his hand back.* Comp. Moses at Rephidim (Ex. xvii. 12).

Utterly destroyed. The Hebrew verb of *cherem.*

VER. 29. *A tree.* Lit., " *the* tree," *i.e.*, the execution-tree, the prepared gallows. The phrase is used for crucifying, impaling, and hanging. It is probable that the king of Ai was slain with the sword and then hanged upon a gallows. It was designed that Israel should count all Canaanites as utterly defiled, and hence every means was taken to express their defilement. (See Appendix.)

Until eventide. See Deut. xxi. 22, 23.
Heap of stones. See on chap. vii. 26.

4. *The Covenant renewed at Shechem.*

VER. 30–35. It has been earnestly contended
that these verses are out of place, and should come
in after the eleventh chapter, when the whole land
had been conquered. The only external evidence
in favor of any displacement is in the fact that in
the LXX these verses are inserted after the second
verse of the next chapter, but that slight alteration
of place does not touch the argument for the trans-
fer to chap. xi. We can see no substantial reason
for supposing any error in the present order. The
fall of Ai, with all that had preceded it at Jordan
and Jericho, had paralyzed the entire people of
Canaan, and had made the time most fitting for
the entire mass of Israel to move up from the
Jordan valley to the exact centre of the land,
which Moses had designated as the place where
Israel should consecrate the land and themselves
to Jehovah. (See Deut. chap. xxvii.) From
Jericho, by Ai and the Mukhna, to Gerizim is a
distance of thirty-three miles, and by the Ghor to
Wady Ahmar, and thence by what we may call the
high road to Gerizim, is a distance of less than
thirty miles. The whole host of Israel could have
made that journey in three days. Moreover, if we
look over the list of kings whom Joshua conquered,
as given in the twelfth chapter, we find that,
between Ai and the great plain of Esdraelon or

4*   F

30 ¶ Then Joshua built an altar unto the LORD
God of Israel in mount Ebal,
31 As Moses the servant of the LORD commanded
the children of Israel, as it is written in the book of the
law of Moses, an altar of whole stones, over which no
man hath lifted up *any* iron: and they offered thereon
burnt-offerings unto the LORD, and sacrificed peace-
offerings.

Jezreel, there were *none*, showing that by some
providential calamity (referred to in Deut. vii. 20,
and Josh. xxiv. 12, as " the hornet ") that central
portion of the land had been stripped of its inhabitants in preparation for Israel's solemn service at
Gerizim and Ebal.

VER. 30. *Then, i.e.,* after the fall of Ai.   The
details of the altar are given in the directions in
Deut. xxvii.   The altar was to be built of great
unhewn stones, and then a coating of plaster was
to be put upon them, on which were to be written
all the words of the first twenty-six chapters of
Deuteronomy.   On this altar, which was to be
erected on Mount Ebal, peace offerings were to
be offered, as well as the burnt offerings.

Mount Ebal stands north of Mount Gerizim, a
very narrow valley running between, in which is
squeezed the modern Nablus, the ancient Shechem.
This valley runs eastward into the north-western
corner of the striking and beautiful plain of
Mukhna.   Mount Gerizim is 2,650, and Mount
Ebal 2,700 feet above the Mediterranean, but they
are not much more than 1,000 feet above the valley.
If you draw a line from the latitude of Sidon to
the latitude of (the supposed) Kadesh-barnea, these

32 ¶ And he wrote there upon the stones a copy of the law of Moses, which he wrote in the presence of the children of Israel.

33 And all Israel, and their elders, and officers, and their judges, stood on this side the ark and on that side before the priests the Levites, which bare the ark of the covenant of the LORD, as well the stranger, as he that was born among them ; half of them over against mount Gerizim, and half of them over against mount Ebal; as Moses the servant of the LORD had commanded before, that they should bless the people of Israel.

mountains are exactly at the half-way point. If you draw another line from the Mediterranean Sea to the top of the Gilead range, again these mountains are at the half-way point. Thus the spot taken for this grand ceremony was exactly in the centre of the new country of the tribes.

VER. 32. *A copy of the law of Moses, which he wrote in the presence of the children of Israel.* This should read, " the second of the law," &c., *i.e.*, Deuteronomy. This was the law which Moses wrote " in the presence of the children of Israel." It was probably the first twenty-six chapters, including all that was written up to the blessings and curses, as law to be read. (See Deut. xxvii. 3, 8.) The other chapters, however, may also be included.

VER. 33. *The priests the Levites.* (See in chap. iii. 3.)

The stranger. Of course, the proselyte. (See Deut. xxxi. 12.)

Should bless. The word " barak " seems to be used here in its double meaning of both blessing and cursing. Six tribes on the Gerizim side were

34 And afterward he read all the words of the law, the blessings and cursings, according to all that is written in the book of the law.

35 There was not a word of all that Moses commanded, which Joshua read not before all the congregation of Israel, with the women, and the little ones, and the strangers that were conversant among them.

to bless the people, and the other six on the Ebal side were to utter the curses (Deut. xxvii. 12, 13).

Ver. 34. Joshua seems to have been preceded by the Levites (Deut. xxvii. 14), who uttered the curses. Then he read aloud the blessings and curses of the twenty-eighth chapter of Deuteronomy. The six tribes on either side may have only symbolically represented the blessings and curses, or may have repeated them after Joshua, or only have responded " amen " to them. It is hard to understand exactly how six of them were " to bless the people," and the other six were " for a cursing."

JOSHUA, CHAP. IX.   85

CHAPTER IX.

1 AND it came to pass, when all the kings which *were* on this side Jordan, in the hills, and in the valleys, and in all the coasts of the great sea over against Lebanon, the Hittite, and the Amorite, the Canaanite, the Perizzite, the Hivite, and the Jebusite heard *thereof;*

5. *The Craft of the Gibeonites.*

VER. 1. *On this side Jordan.* Lit., "beyond Jordan." They were "beyond Jordan" to Israel's start in the invasion, *i.e.*, to the Moabitish country.

In the hills. The mountain region, or backbone of Palestine, known afterward as the hill-country of Judah, Mount Ephraim, &c.

In the valleys. Heb., "in the Shephelah," the name especially given to the great Philistine plain. It is from a root which means "low."

In all the coasts of the great sea over against Lebanon. The strip of low coast land from Carmel to Ras en-Nakura. The Girgashite is left out of this list. The Jewish tradition, sustained by Procopius, is that they fled the country on Joshua's approach and settled in north-western Africa. Josh. xxiv. 11, shows that if they did thus flee, they fought against Israel with the other tribes of Canaan before their flight.

2 That they gathered themselves together, to fight with Joshua and with Israel, with one accord.

3 ¶ And when the inhabitants of Gibeon heard what Joshua had done unto Jericho and to Ai,

VER. 2. This gathering was a reaction after the paralysis caused by the destruction of Jericho and Ai. It may have been consummated as much as a month after the taking of Ai.

VER. 3. *Gibeon* is afraid to enter into the confederacy. It was the head city of a Hivite tetra-

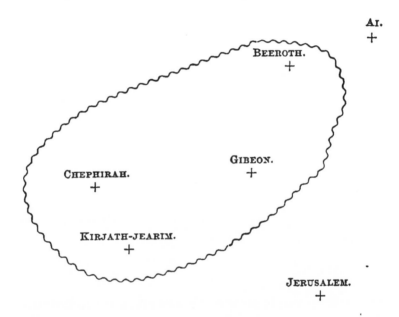

polis, to wit, Gibeon, Chephirah, Beeroth, and Kirjath-jearim (ver. 17), forming a republic or oligarchy in the midst of the monarchies of Palestine. On this account it was easier and more natural for Gibeon to act independently of the other principalities. *Gibeon* was only a little more

4 They did work wilily, and went and made as if
they had been ambassadors, and took old sacks upon
their asses, and wine-bottles, old, and rent, and
bound up;

than six miles south-west of Ai. *Chephirah* was
five and a half miles west of Gibeon. *Beeroth*
was four miles north of Gibeon. *Kirjath-jearim*
was about five miles south-west of Gibeon, and
two and a half miles south of Chephirah. The
sites of all these places are identified.

The sketch on page 86 shows the proportionate
relations in distance and direction between the Gibeonite cities, Ai and Jerusalem. Beeroth, one of
their cities, was only three miles from Ai. The district of the Gibeonite tetrapolis would be about
eleven miles in length and half that in breadth.
The nearest royal town to the district (after Ai
and Bethel) would be Jerusalem, not much more
than five miles from Gibeon.

VER. 4. *They did work wilily.* Lit., " they also
wrought with craft." That is, these Gibeonites,
like all the other inhabitants of Canaan, wrought
against Israel; but while the others did it with
arms, these did it with craft. It shows that there
was no recognition of Jehovah (as in Rahab's case),
but simply a cunning act to overreach Joshua.
Rahab's example would, doubtless, have been
followed by Rahab's sequel. But the Gibeonites
became servants, while Rahab became the ances-
tress of David and Christ. There is a close connection between second and third verses.

Wine-bottles. Rather, " skins of wine."

5 And old shoes and clouted upon their feet, and old garments upon them; and all the bread of their provision was dry *and* mouldy.

6 And they went to Joshua unto the camp at Gilgal, and said unto him, and to the men of Israel. We be come from a far country; now therefore make ye a league with us.

VER. 5. *Clouted, i.e.*, patched.

Mouldy. Lit., " speckled."

VER. 6. *Gilgal.* This could not be the Gilgal down by Jordan, so far away from the centre to which Joshua had penetrated; but the Gilgal of 2 Kings ii. 1, which was higher than Bethel (2 Kings ii. 2). It is this second Gilgal which, we think, became so famous in Samuel's day, and which became a centre of idolatry. (See 1 Sam. vii. 16, x. 8, xi. 14, xiii. 7, 8, xv. 33; Hos. iv. 15, ix. 15, xii. 11; Amos iv. 4, v. 5.) It was the great head-quarters of Israel, until the tabernacle was pitched at Shiloh, which was not far off. Hence it became a place of traditional sanctity to after generations, and idolatry readily erected there one of its shrines, as at Bethel. This view is taken by Keil, and his arguments are convincing. Van de Velde holds the same. This second Gilgal bears still the old name (Jiljilieh), and is situated on a commanding height fifteen miles due north of Jerusalem, three miles west of the high northern road, and about seven miles north and west of Ai. It is also about fourteen miles south of Mount Gerizim. " It is near the western brow of the high mountain tract, and affords an exten-

7 And the men of Israel said unto the Hivites, Peradventure ye dwell among us; and how shall we make a league with you?

8 And they said unto Joshua, We *are* thy servants. And Joshua said unto them, Who *are* ye? and from whence come ye?

9 And they said unto him, From a very far country thy servants are come, because of the name of the LORD thy God: for we have heard the fame of him, and all that he did in Egypt,

10 And all that he did to the two kings of the Amorites, that *were* beyond Jordan, to Sihon king of Heshbon, and to Og king of Bashan, which *was* at Ashtaroth.

11 Wherefore our elders, and all the inhabitants of

sive view over the great lower plain and the sea, while at the same time the mountains of Gilead are seen in the east." (Robinson.) It also has distant Hermon in sight. No more suitable spot could have been selected for Israel's central post during the process of the conquest.

VER. 7. *Peradventure ye dwell among us; and how shall we make a league with you?* (See Ex. xxiii. 32; Deut. vii. 2, xx. 16.) No league could be made with the people of Canaan. But this does not forbid the accepting any as proselytes. There may have been many such, like Rahab's family.

VER. 8. *We are thy servants.* A formula of oriental politeness.

VER. 9, 10. *All that he did in Egypt, and all that he did to the two kings of the Amorites.* They adroitly say nothing of the crossing of the Jordan, or of Jericho and Ai, as if these later matters had not reached their distant home when they left.

our country spake to us, saying, Take victuals with you for the journey, and go to meet them, and say unto them, We *are* your servants: therefore now make ye a league with us:

12 This our bread we took hot *for* our provision out of our houses on the day we came forth to go unto you; but now, behold, it is dry, and it is mouldy:

13 And these bottles of wine which we filled, *were* new, and behold they be rent: and these our garments and our shoes are become old by reason of the very long journey.

14 And the men took of their victuals, and asked not *counsel* at the mouth of the LORD.

15 And Joshua made peace with them, and made a league with them, to let them live: and the princes of the congregation sware unto them.

16 ¶ And it came to pass at the end of three days after they had made a league with them, that they heard that they *were* their neighbours, and *that* they dwelt among them.

17 And the children of Israel journeyed, and came unto their cities on the third day. Now their cities *were* Gibeon, and Chephirah, and Beeroth, and Kirjath-jearim.

18 And the children of Israel smote them not, be-

VER. 14. Read, according to the margin, *they received the men by reason of their victuals, and asked not counsel at the mouth of the Lord.* They judged the case for themselves, and the mouldy bread was the criterion, when, in such an emergency, they should have applied to the Urim and Thummim.

VER. 17. *On the third day.* That is the same as "at the end of three days," in ver. 16. The armed men would move from Gilgal to Gibeon (about twelve miles) in the same day on which the news was heard.

VER. 18. The congregation, remembering Achan's

cause the princes of the congregation had sworn unto
them by the LORD God of Israel. And all the congregation murmured against the princes.

19 But all the princes said unto all the congregation,
We have sworn unto them by the LORD God of Israel:
now therefore we may not touch them.

20 This we will do to them; we will even let them
live, lest wrath be upon us, because of the oath which
we sware unto them.

21 And the princes said unto them, Let them live;
but let them be hewers of wood, and drawers of water
unto all the congregation; as the princes had promised
them.

sin and its dreadful consequences, would naturally
fear that a new sin and judgment were here presented.

VER. 19. *We may not touch them.* " Touch " in
the sense of " slay " or " smite." So the Heb.

VER. 20. *Lest wrath be upon us.* They show
the people (through their representatives) that
God's wrath, which, the people feared, would be
experienced if the solemn oath was broken.

VER. 21. They will make, however, a clear indication of their sense of error, and will degrade the
Hivites to be menial servants to the congregation.
The sin of the princes was not in keeping the
oath, but in making it. (Comp. Ps. xv. 4.) Jehovah's holy name was to be honored among the
heathen by Israel's keeping the oath uttered to
him. God, by his dealing with Saul's family for
their slaughter of some of the Gibeonites four
hundred years later (2 Sam. xxi.), puts the
seal of his approbation on this decision of the
princes to keep the oath.

92 COMMENTARY ON

22 ¶ And Joshua called for them, and he spake unto them, saying, Wherefore have ye beguiled us, saying, We *are* very far from you; when ye dwell among us?

23 Now therefore ye *are* cursed, and there shall none of you be freed from being bond-men, and hewers of wood and drawers of water for the house of my God.

24 And they answered Joshua, and said, Because it was certainly told thy servants, how that the LORD thy God commanded his servant Moses to give you all the land, and to destroy all the inhabitants of the land from before you, therefore we were sore afraid of our lives because of you, and have done this thing.

25 And now, behold, we *are* in thine hand: as it seemeth good and right unto thee to do unto us, do.

26 And so did he unto them, and delivered them out of the hand of the children of Israel, that they slew them not.

27 And Joshua made them that day hewers of wood and drawers of water for the congregation and for the altar of the LORD, even unto this day, in the place which he should choose.

VER. 22. *Joshua called for them.* The representative army of Israel, with Joshua at its head, had moved to Gibeon, and there Joshua probably summons the representatives of the four cities and tells them the decision of Israel concerning them.

VER. 23. *Cursed.* Heb., " arar," and not " charam " (whence *cherem*).

For the house of my God. They were to be public tabernacle menials, and not private slaves.

VER. 27. *Hewers of wood and drawers of water.* In this low position, and under constant ecclesiastical oversight, they would not tempt the people of Israel to Canaanitish sins. All open idolatries would be prevented. Doubtless their descendants became thoroughly attached to the Jewish system. It is generally supposed that the *Neth-*

inim of later days (1 Chron. ix. 2; Ezra ii. 43, &c.) were the Gibeonites, so called from the word *nathan* (to give), used by Joshua in this verse, " and Joshua made them that day," &c. (lit., " and Joshua *gave* them that day," &c.).

CHAPTER X.

1 Now it came to pass, when Adoni-zedek king of Jerusalem had heard how Joshua had taken Ai, and had utterly destroyed it; as he had done to Jericho and her king, so he had done to Ai and her king; and how the inhabitants of Gibeon had made peace with Israel, and were among them;

2 That they feared greatly, because Gibeon *was* a great city, as one of the royal cities, and because it *was* greater than Ai, and all the men thereof *were* mighty.

3 Wherefore Adoni-zedek king of Jerusalem sent unto Hoham king of Hebron, and unto Piram king of Jarmuth, and unto Japhia king of Lachish, and unto Debir king of Eglon, saying,

6. *The Conquest of the South.*

VER. 1. *Adoni-zedek.* This name (lord of righteousness), so like to Melchi-zedek (king of righteousness), mentioned in Gen. xiv. 18, as King of Salem, has suggested the prevailing idea that Salem and Jerusalem are the same, and that its kings for five centuries had borne the title of Melchi-zedek, or Adoni-zedek. As the distance of time is so great, it may be only a coincidence that the word *zedek* should appear in both these proper names.

VER. 2. *As one of the royal cities.* That is, although it had no king, but was one of a confederacy of republican towns, yet it had the power and importance of one of the cities that had a king.

VER. 3. *Hebron, Jarmuth, Lachish,* and *Eglon*

4 Come up unto me, and help me, that we may smite
Gibeon: for it hath made peace with Joshua and with
the children of Israel.

were probably the largest, strongest, and most
important cities of southern Canaan, and hence
the king of Jerusalem, the nearest royal city to
Joshua's host, sends to them for a union of forces.
He was cut off from all the northern kings by
Joshua's army.

Hebron is nineteen miles south of Jerusalem, on
the highest portion of the mountain country. It
was the old Abrahamic home, and in its immediate
vicinity was the cave of Machpelah (Gen. xxiii. 19).
The Hittites occupied it in Abraham's day, but
now it appears the Amorites (ver. 5) held it.
Afterward, between Joshua's capture of it (ver.
37) and Caleb's occupation of it (chap. xi. 21,
and chap. xv. 13), the Anakim dwelt there.

Jarmuth is sixteen miles south of west of Jerusalem, on the slope of the mountain country, and
about eight miles from the Shephelah, or Philistine
plain. It is fifteen miles from Hebron.

Lachish was a very famous town in later days,
as seen by its mention in Assyrian records, thirty-
six miles south-west of Jerusalem, on the Shephelah, and fourteen miles from Gaza.

Eglon was only three miles east of Lachish, and
twenty-five miles west of Hebron.

VER. 4. *That we may smite Gibeon.* Although
Gibeon was their object, they must have known
that Israel would be also met. But Israel's name

5 Therefore the five kings of the Amorites, the king of Jerusalem, the king of Hebron, the king of Jarmuth, the king of Lachish, the king of Eglon, gathered themselves together, and went up, they and all their hosts, and encamped before Gibeon, and made war against it.

6 ¶ And the men of Gibeon sent unto Joshua to the camp to Gilgal, saying, Slack not thy hand from thy servants; come up to us quickly, and save us, and help us: for all the kings of the Amorites that dwell in the mountains are gathered together against us.

7 So Joshua ascended from Gilgal, he, and all the people of war with him, and all the mighty men of valour.

8 ¶ And the LORD said unto Joshua, Fear them not:

had become so formidable, that it was policy for Adoni-zedek not to use it, but to use the name of Gibeon only in forming the league.

VER. 6. *Gilgal.* See chap. ix. 6.

The kings of the Amorites that dwell in the mountains. Probably these five kings possessed most of the mountain-country south of Gibeon, although two of their capitals, Lachish and Eglon, were down in the great plain.

VER. 7. *Ascended.* Although the mountain Gilgal (chap. ix. 6) is situated on high ground, yet the land rises as you go south from it to Gibeon.

And all the mighty men of valour. It was customary in ancient armies to have a select force of the most valiant reserved for special occasions. Such were Xerxes' " immortals." These " mighty men of valour " seem to have been such a select battalion. Joshua foresaw that a great and decisive battle was at hand.

VER. 8. A new strengthening of Joshua's heart

for I have delivered them into thine hand; there shall not a man of them stand before thee.

9 Joshua therefore came unto them suddenly, *and* went up from Gilgal all night.

10 And the Lord discomfited them before Israel, and slew them with a great slaughter at Gibeon, and chased them along the way that goeth up to Beth-horon, and smote them to Azekah, and unto Makkedah.

is given by God, probably through the high-priest and the Urim.

Ver. 9. *Joshua therefore.* Notice how the " therefore " is introduced. The word is not in the Hebrew, but it is implied. Joshua, when assured of success, uses every precaution. This is the process of a true faith.

All night. They could easily reach Gibeon (twelve miles from Gilgal) in one night.

Ver. 10. The great battle was fought on the beautiful basin below the hill of Gibeon, and on its west side. The pursuit was down the remarkable pass of Beth-horon.

Azekah and *Makkedah,* although not identified, are generally supposed to be near Wady Sumt, and in the neighborhood of Jarmuth. (The kings, after reaching the plain, would flee toward their cities.) If so, the pursuit must have been for thirty miles from the battle-field. We must give at least ten hours for this. If the battle were joined at six in the morning, and speedily decided by the flight of the Amorites, we cannot put the arrival at Makkedah of the pursued and pursuers before five o'clock in the afternoon. Now, if we are to take " that day " in ver. 28 literally,

5   G

> 11 And it came to pass as they fled from before Israel, *and* were in the going down to Beth-horon, that the LORD cast down great stones from heaven upon them unto Azekah, and they died: *they were* more which died with hailstones than *they* whom the children of Israel slew with the sword.

then the capture of Makkedah must have been in the evening of that same eventful day. But we need not press that phrase. " That day " may signify " at that juncture," or, generally, " at that time."

VER. 11. *The going down to Beth-horon.* This is the remarkable pass between Beit Ur el-Tahta and Beit Ur el-Foka, lying west from Gibeon.

Unto Azekah. As Azekah was one of the termini of the flight, the miraculous hail-storm followed the pursued for nearly the whole of the long flight, while Israel followed in safety.

VER. 12–14. These verses have given rise to a great amount of adverse criticism. Some rejecting them as an interpolation, others considering them as a mere quotation from an imaginative poem, and still others using them as arguments against the truth of the Scriptures. The fact that it is introduced after the description of the flight to Azekah does not prove it an interpolation. That manner of writing an historical narrative is eminently Hebraic. It is not a *mere* quotation, but, if there is a quotation, it is followed by the sacred writer's endorsement in verses 13 and 14. And why should not God, through Joshua, perform this miracle, as well as that of the stopping of the tem-

12 ¶ Then spake Joshua to the LORD in the day when the LORD delivered up the Amorites before the children of Israel, and he said in the sight of Israel, Sun, stand thou still upon Gibeon, and thou Moon, in the valley of Ajalon.

pest on the lake of Galilee, or that of bringing the shadow ten degrees backward on the dial of Ahaz? (2 Ki. xx. 11). The favorite argument of the sceptic is founded on the fact that the command for the sun to stand still implies a false view of the motions of the heavenly bodies. This objection is very puerile in any one who daily talks of the sun *rising* and *setting*. The language, "stand still," is phenomenal, and the phenomenon may have occurred by some action of God through the laws of refraction.

VER. 12. *Sun — upon Gibeon — moon, in the valley of Ajalon.* Gibeon was east of the battle-field, Ajalon was west. So it must have been in the morning,* at the beginning of the flight, say at seven o'clock, that the sun and moon were ordered to occupy their present positions (phenomenally). This command was made known to the army (*in the sight of Israel*), and its fulfilment must have been a grand encouragement all that day. When the final scene occurred at Makkedah, at (say) five o'clock in the afternoon, then, if not before, the refraction may have ceased and the two heavenly bodies

---

* It must have been several days after full moon, probably the first full moon after the passover at Gilgal; that is, about five weeks after that passover, and in the sixth week after crossing the Jordan.

13 And the sun stood still, and the moon stayed, until the people had avenged themselves upon their enemies. *Is* not this written in the book of Jasher? So the sun stood still in the midst of heaven, and hasted not to go down about a whole day.

14 And there was no day like that before it or after it, that the LORD hearkened unto the voice of a man: for the LORD fought for Israel.

taken their normal phenomenal relation to Israel, the moon having disappeared and the sun shining forth from the western horizon. It does not appear that the day was lengthened, but only that these two heavenly bodies seemed motionless for many hours. " The sun stood still in the midst (or ' the half part ') of heaven," *i.e.*, did not cross over to the other half, " and hasted not to go down *like a complete day*." The Hebrew as naturally takes this meaning as "about a whole day." In the ordering of the miracle, note that " Joshua spoke to the Lord." The command was an inspired prayer. (See Appendix.)

VER. 14. There was no such day, as the result of the Lord's hearing man's prayer. This is the meaning of this verse. The Lord often heard and answered prayer by miraculous interference before this and after this, but he never before or after so marked the day in its aspect as he did this, at the prayer of man. The Book of Jasher (or " the Upright One ") is mentioned also in 2 Sam. i. 18, and was, perhaps, one of the sacred poems which God, in his providence, has caused to disappear. There are other books, like those of Iddo, of Gad, &c., referred to in the Scriptures which may have

15 ¶ And Joshua returned, and all Israel with him, unto the camp to Gilgal.

16 But these five kings fled, and hid themselves in a cave at Makkedah.

17 And it was told Joshua, saying, The five kings are found hid in a cave at Makkedah.

18 And Joshua said, Roll great stones upon the mouth of the cave, and set men by it for to keep them:

19 And stay ye not, *but* pursue after your enemies, and smite the hindmost of them; suffer them not to enter into their cities: for the LORD your God hath delivered them into your hand.

20 And it came to pass, when Joshua and the children of Israel had made an end of slaying them with a very great slaughter, till they were consumed, that the rest *which* remained of them entered into fenced cities.

21 And all the people returned to the camp to Joshua at Makkedah in peace: none moved his tongue against any of the children of Israel.

served their purpose prior to the Babylonian captivity, and were then lost. They may have been inspired works.

VER. 15. This verse is not out of place,* but the narrative ends here, and then is resumed in ver. 16, in order to describe the sequel of the battle of Gibeon. This is the Hebraic style of writing. The verse is then repeated at ver. 43.

VER. 17. *In a cave at Makkedah.* Summeil, on the great plain by Wady Sumt, which Van de Velde considers Makkedah, has a very remarkable cave in its immediate vicinity. The word here has the definite article, *the cave at Makkedah.*

VER. 21. *None· moved his tongue.* The defeat of the confederate kings had been so thorough, the

* To make it part of the extract from the Book of Jasher is most unnecessary and harsh.

22 Then said Joshua, Open the mouth of the cave, and bring out those five kings unto me out of the cave.

23 And they did so, and brought forth those five kings unto him out of the cave, the king of Jerusalem, the king of Hebron, the king of Jarmuth, the king of Lachish, *and* the king of Eglon.

24 And it came to pass, when they brought out those kings unto Joshua, that Joshua called for all the men of Israel, and said unto the captains of the men of war which went with him, Come near, put your feet upon the necks of these kings. And they came near, and put their feet upon the necks of them.

25 And Joshua said unto them, Fear not, nor be dismayed, be strong and of good courage: for thus shall the LORD do to all your enemies against whom ye fight.

26 And afterward Joshua smote them, and slew them, and hanged them on five trees: and they were hanging upon the trees until the evening.

27 And it came to pass at the time of the going down of the sun, *that* Joshua commanded, and they

entire land ceased to offer further offensive opposition.

VER. 24. *All the men of Israel, i.e.*, all the Israelitish army.

Put your feet upon the necks of these kings. A significant Oriental act to encourage Israel, a visible pledge that they should conquer all their foes.

VER. 25. *Fear not*, &c. Joshua thus reassures Israel, who had probably never fully regained confidence since the disaster before Ai.

VER. 26. The hanging was a mark of cursing from God, an exhibition of their own stewardship under him. (See Deut. xxi. 23.)

Until the evening. (See the verse above cited from Deuteronomy.)

VER. 27. *Until the very day.* (See note on chap. vii. 26.)

took them down off the trees, and cast them into the cave wherein they had been hid, and laid great stones in the cave's mouth, *which remain* until this very day.

28 ¶ And that day Joshua took Makkedah, and smote it with the edge of the sword, and the king thereof he utterly destroyed, them, and all the souls that *were* therein ; he let none remain : and he did to the king of Makkedah as he did unto the king of Jericho.

29 Then Joshua passed from Makkedah, and all Israel with him, unto Libnah, and fought against Libnah:

30 And the LORD delivered it also, and the king thereof, into the hand of Israel: and he smote it with the edge of the sword, and all the souls that *were* therein; he let none remain in it ; but did unto the king thereof as he did unto the king of Jericho.

31 ¶ And Joshua passed from Libnah, and all Israel with him, unto Lachish, and encamped against it, and fought against it.

32 And the LORD delivered Lachish into the hand of Israel, which took it on the second day, and smote it with the edge of the sword, and all the souls that *were* therein, according to all that he had done to Libnah.

33 ¶ Then Horam king of Gezer came up to help Lachish; and Joshua smote him and his people, until he had left him none remaining.

VER. 28. *That day.* (See note on ver. 10.)

VER. 29. *Libnah* is conjectured by Van de Velde to be at Arak-el-Menshiyeh on Wady Safieh, five miles from his supposed site of Makkedah.

VER. 31. *Lachish.* (See note on ver. 3.)

VER. 33. Gezer is the first city that attempts voluntarily to withstand the tide of Israel's conquests. The king had, perhaps, supposed that at so strong a spot as Lachish a successful resistance could be made, and hence offered to reinforce the king of Lachish. Joshua, after destroying Lachish, did not go to Gezer, but to Eglon. The king of

34 ¶ And from Lachish Joshua passed unto Eglon, and all Israel with him: and they encamped against it, and fought against it:

35 And they took it on that day, and smote it with the edge of the sword, and all the souls that *were* therein he utterly destroyed that day, according to all that he had done to Lachish.

36 And Joshua went up from Eglon, and all Israel with him, unto Hebron; and they fought against it:

37 And they took it, and smote it with the edge of the sword, and the king thereof, and all the cities thereof, and all the souls that *were* therein; he left none remaining, according to all that he had done to Eglon, but destroyed it utterly, and all the souls that *were* therein.

38 ¶ And Joshua returned, and all Israel with him, to Debir; and fought against it:

39 And he took it, and the king thereof, and all the cities thereof, and they smote them with the edge of the sword, and utterly destroyed all the souls that *were* therein; he left none remaining : as he had done to Hebron, so he did to Debir, and to the king thereof; as he had done also to Libnah, and to her king.

40 ¶ So Joshua smote all the country of the hills,

Gezer and his army were slain at Lachish. Gezer was thirty miles north of Lachish, and near Joppa.

VER. 34. *Eglon.* (See note on ver. 3.)

VER. 36. *Hebron.* (See note on ver. 3.)

VER. 37. *The king thereof.* They had a new king at Hebron, after the death of the former king at Makkedah.

VER. 38. *Debir.* Dr. Rosen identifies Debir with Dewir-ban, a few miles west of Hebron; but the requirements of the grouping in chap. xv. 49, would place it farther south. Debir was afterward reconquered by Othniel (Judg. i. 11, 12).

VER. 40. *The hills,* i.e., the mountain-country; *the south,* i.e., the Negeb, or land on the southern

and of the south, and of the vale, and of the springs, and all their kings: he left none remaining, but utterly destroyed all that breathed, as the LORD God of Israel commanded.

41 And Joshua smote them from Kadesh-barnea even unto Gaza, and all the country of Goshen, even unto Gibeon.

42 And all these kings and their land did Joshua take at one time ; because the LORD God of Israel fought for Israel.

43 And Joshua returned, and all Israel with him, unto the camp to Gilgal.

slopes toward the desert; *the vale, i.e.,* the Shephelah or Philistine plain; *the springs, i.e.,* the ravines on the borders between the mountain-country and the Shephelah.

All that breathed, i.e., all the human beings whom he found. Many escaped to hiding-places, and afterward came out and fought Israel, as the Anakim at Hebron and Kirjath-sepher (or Debir), who reconquered those towns.

As the Lord God of Israel commanded. There is the foundation of the whole conquest and all its details. It was not man's doing, and is not to be so judged.

VER. 41. *Kadesh-barnea* is often spoken of as the limit of Palestine to the south. Some would put it near the Arabah, south of the Dead Sea, and others far to the west of the Arabah. We cannot be sure of its exact site, but may place it with much probability on a line of latitude at least twenty miles south of the Dead Sea. *Gaza* is a well-known site on the Mediterranean, fifty miles south-west of Jerusalem. *Goshen* was prob-

5*

ably the name given to the southern portion of the mountain-region south of Hebron, between Hebron and the Negeb. It may have some connection with the Egyptian Goshen. Perhaps Israel gave it that name in memory of their Egyptian home. The region here given as conquered by Joshua in this southern campaign is about eighty miles from Gibeon southward, and sixty miles from the Mediterranean to the Dead Sea and Arabah. We may suppose several months or even a year to have been spent in this campaign.

CHAPTER XI.

1 AND it came to pass, when Jabin king of Hazor had heard *those things;* that he sent to Jobab king of Madon, and to the king of Shimron, and to the king of Achshaph,

7. *The Conquest of the North.*

VER. 1. *Jabin king of Hazor.* More than a century later another king of this name and place appears (Judg. iv. 2). He made an unsuccessful though formidable attempt to reconstruct the Canaanitish rule, holding nearly all Israel under his sway or fear for twenty years.

Hazor (as we see by ver. 10) was the chief city of the north, and hence its king was leader of the northern confederation or alliance. It is doubtful where the town stood. Robinson thinks very near to the Huleh. Knobel puts it fifteen miles farther west, half-way across the country toward the ladder of Tyre, at Huzzur, which is more likely.

Madon cannot be identified. Why its king should be named, as is the king of Hazor, and the names of the other kings be suppressed, is only to be explained by supposing Jabin and Jobab to be men of remarkable distinction in statesmanship or war.

> 2 And to the kings that *were* on the north of the
> mountains, and of the plains south of Cinneroth, and
> in the valley, and in the borders of Dor on the west,

Shimron (Shimron-meron in chap. xii. 20) is
identified by the Talmud with Semmunieh, five
miles west of Nazareth.

Achshaph cannot be identified; but Grove's
suggestion of Haifa on the bay of Akka is a good
one. I would suggest Iksim, near Tantara.

VER. 2. *The kings that were on the north of the
mountains.* Rather, *the kings that were on the north
in the mountain country*, that is, the kings north of
Joshua's northmost position at Mount Ebal, whose
cities were in the central mountain region of Galilee.

And of the plains south of Chinneroth. Rather,
and in the Arabah south of Chinneroth, that is, in
the Ghor or Jordan depression, south of the lake
of Galilee; for Chinnereth, or Chinneroth, was the
town whence the lake derived its name, and is used
here for the lake itself.

And in the valley. Lit., *and in the Shephelah*,
i.e., the Philistine plain, referring to the northern
part between the Nahr el-Aujeh and the Nahr
Akhdar.

And in the borders of Dor. Rather, *and in the
highlands of Dor.* From the Nahr Akhdar northward the country between the Carmel range and
the sea is no longer the Shephelah or low plain,
but a region of hills. They are here called from
the city on the coast "the highlands of Dor."

3 *And to* the Canaanite on the east and on the west,
and *to* the Amorite, and the Hittite, and the Perizzite,
and the Jebusite in the mountains, and *to* the Hivite
under Hermon in the land of Mizpeh.

4 And they went out, they and all their hosts with
them, much people, even as the sand that *is* upon the
sea-shore in multitude, with horses and chariots very
many.

5 And when all these kings were met together, they
came and pitched together at the waters of Merom, to
fight against Israel.

VER. 3. *And to* should be omitted. The enumeration of this verse is in apposition with the
foregoing. The Canaanite on east and west were
the inhabitants of the Shephelah, the Ghor and
the heights of Dor already referred to ; and the
Amorites, Hittites, Perizzites, and Jebusites in
the mountains were the inhabitants of the mountains already referred to ; while *the Hivite beneath
Hermon in the land of Mizpeh* was the population
of the extreme north of Galilee, where the mountain-region of Galilee begins to change into the
lofty ranges of Lebanon. The lofty country between the Leontes and the Jordan would exactly
suit this description, as *beneath Hermon*, and as a
land of Mizpeh (outlook). The Girgashite is omitted in this enumeration. (See note on chap. ix. 1.)

VER. 5. *The waters of Merom* have been generally supposed to be the same as Lake Semechonitis,
or the Huleh, but Keil suggests that they are the
waters of Wady Tawham, which flow down from
the present village of Meiron, a few miles west of
Safed, into the lake of Galilee. There is another
" Maron " ten miles west of the Huleh, which has

6 ¶ And the LORD said unto Joshua, Be not afraid
because of them: for to-morrow about this time will I
deliver them up all slain before Israel: thou shalt hough
their horses, and burn their chariots with fire.

equal claims. Eusebius puts Merom at twelve
miles from Samaria and near Dothan. This would
agree with the southern border of the great plain
of Esdraelon ; and as this was the natural spot to
check an army advancing from the south, I am
inclined to place this battle-field of Jabin in the
neighborhood of Megiddo, and to make the waters
of Merom identical with the waters of Megiddo
(Judges v. 19). This was the spot where the
second Jabin was overcome by Barak, and where
Josiah fought his fatal battle with Necho (2 Ki.
xxiii. 29). In such a spot they could use chariots,
but in the other sites assumed it would be almost
impossible.

VER. 6. *Be not afraid.* This is the fourth time
that by these words God directly encouraged his
faithful servant: first, when he succeeded to
Moses' responsibility (chap. i. 6, 7, 9) ; secondly,
when after Achan's sin and its sad results a new
movement was to be made (chap. viii. 1) ; thirdly,
when the southern alliance was formed against
Israel (chap. x. 8) ; and now, fourthly, when the
northern alliance is formed. We may add as anal-
ogous the words given by God in his appearance
as a warrior to Joshua before the capture of Jericho (chap. vi. 2), although this special formula is
not used. (See note on chap. i. 6.)

7 So Joshua came, and all the people of war with him, against them by the waters of Merom suddenly, and they fell upon them.

8 And the LORD delivered them into the hand of Israel, who smote them, and chased them unto great Zidon, and unto Misrephoth-maim, and unto the val-

Thou shalt hough their horses. To "hough" is to "hamstring." But this Hebrew word " akar " is used in 2 Sam. viii. 4, and in 1 Chron. xviii. 4, of chariots ("horses" are inserted in the English version), and in Zeph. ii. 4, it is used (in a paronomasia it is true) of the city of Ekron. In the passage in Gen. xlix. 6, if we read *shur* instead of *shor* (as is done by some, and as seems to be the most probable reading), the word *akar* is used of a wall. The word seems to be of the same stock with *achar* (compare the roots *kanan* and *chanan*, and many other examples), and the primary idea appears to be " to strike " or " to smite." Proof is wanting that the ordinary translation of " hough " is a correct one. It would have been a difficult and useless task to hamstring an enemy's horse in battle, when a blow on the head or body would be easy and efficacious. And, moreover, there would have been a cruelty in it utterly at war with the kindly care enjoined upon the Jews in the law with respect to dumb animals (Deut. xxv. 4).

VER. 7. *They fell upon them.* With the same suddenness and (as we think) at the same place where Gideon fell upon the Midianites two centuries later (Judg. vii. 21).

VER. 8. *Unto great Zidon, and unto Misrephoth-*

ley of Mizpeh eastward; and they smote them, until
they left them none remaining.

9 And Joshua did unto them as the LORD bade him:
he houghed their horses, and burnt their chariots with
fire.

10 ¶ And Joshua at that time turned back, and
took Hazor, and smote the king thereof with the sword:
for Hazor beforetime was the head of all those kingdoms.

11 And they smote all the souls that *were* therein
with the edge of the sword, utterly destroying *them:*
there was not any left to breathe: and he burnt Hazor
with fire.

maim, and unto the valley of Mizpeh eastward.
Zidon, or Sidon, is called " great," as being at this
time the chief of the coast cities. Tyre afterward
attained to the headship. Sidon is eighty-five
miles from our supposed site of the battle. The
flight of the Canaanites would be into the plain of
Akka, and then along the coast northward.

Misrephoth-maim is placed by Schultz, Thomson,
and Van de Velde at Ain Mesherfi, near the Ladder
of Tyre.

The valley of Mizpeh would be the beautiful
Merj Ayun between the Leontes and the upper
Jordan (Hasbany). See on ver. 3. Part of the
fugitives passed up along the coast to Sidon.
Another part, on reaching the Ladder of Tyre,
turned north-eastwardly along that mountain-wall,
and passed up to the Hermon region.

VER. 10. *Turned back* from the pursuit to Sidon.

Hazor. (See on ver. 1.)

VER. 11. *Burnt Hazor with fire.* In ver. 13
we are told that Hazor was the only city in the

12 And all the cities of those kings, and all the kings of them, did Joshua take, and smote them with the edge of the sword, *and* he utterly destroyed them, as Moses the servant of the LORD commanded.

13 But *as for* the cities that stood still in their strength, Israel burned none of them, save Hazor only; *that* did Joshua burn.

14 And all the spoil of these cities, and the cattle, the children of Israel took for a prey unto themselves: but every man they smote with the edge of the sword, until they had destroyed them, neither left they any to breathe.

15 ¶ As the LORD commanded Moses his servant, so did Moses command Joshua, and so did Joshua: he left nothing undone of all that the LORD commanded Moses.

16 So Joshua took all that land, the hills, and all the south country, and all the land of Goshen, and the valley, and the plain, and the mountain of Israel, and the valley of the same;

northern confederacy that Joshua burned. Its position may have been so strong, or its prestige may have been so great, that, while the conquest was in process, it was wise to wipe the city entirely away.

VER. 12. *As Moses the servant of the Lord commanded.* (Num. xxxiii. 52; Deut. vii. 2, xx. 16, 17.)

VER. 13. *That stood still in their strength.* Rather, *that stood on their hills.* All these towns were built, for strength and security, on hills.

VER. 15. The frequent repetition of God's order is to be carefully noted, as showing that Israel's action was exceptional and no example to men in general, performed solely at God's command.

VER. 16. (See on chap. ix. 1, x. 40, xi. 2.) Joshua captured, — 1, the mountain country;

17 *Even* from the mount Halak, that goeth up to Seir, even unto Baal-gad, in the valley of Lebanon under mount Hermon: and all their kings he took, and smote them, and slew them.

18 Joshua made war a long time with all those kings.

2, the Negeb (south of the mountain country); 3, Goshen (the southern slopes of the mountains). See chap. x. 41; 4, the Shephelah (Philistine country); 5, the Arabah (Jordan and Dead Sea valley); 6, the mountain of Israel (the northern mountains); 7, the northern Shephelah (the upper part of the Shephelah).

VER. 17. *The mount Halak, that goeth up to Seir.* Rather, *the smooth mountain that goeth up to Seir.* Keil's suggestion, that this is the Azazimeh mountain, is a good one. I would, however, take its *southern* edge, and not its northern, as the limit of Israel's conquest. This mountain *goes up to Seir*, because its southern face trends north-eastwardly to the Arabah, where the territory of Seir or Edom begins.

Baal-gad is supposed by Robinson to be Banias, at the source of the eastern branch of the Jordan, the same spot known in the New Testament as Cæsarea Philippi. Van de Velde's suggestion of Bostra or Aisafa, as *in* the valley of Lebanon, is better.

VER. 18. *A long time.* We may suppose a year spent in the general subjugation of the south and a year in the general subjugation of the north, and then a number of years spent in going over

19 There was not a city that made peace with the children of Israel, save the Hivites the inhabitants of Gibeon: all *other* they took in battle.

20 For it was of the LORD to harden their hearts, that they should come against Israel in battle, that he might destroy them utterly, *and* that they might have no favour, but that he might destroy them, as the LORD commanded Moses.

21 ¶ And at that time came Joshua and cut off the Anakims from the mountains, from Hebron, from Debir, from Anab, and from all the mountains of Judah, and from all the mountains of Israel: Joshua destroyed them utterly with their cities.

the same ground more thoroughly. Joshua was seven years subduing the land, as we see from chap. xiv. 7, 10. If he entered Palestine at the age of eighty, and was seven years in subduing the land, he had twenty-three years of peaceful old age.

VER. 20. *It was of the Lord to harden their hearts.* God was, as judge, engaged in punishing this people for their sins. He had withdrawn his grace, and thus hardened their hearts, as the withdrawing of the sun's heat hardens the water. The hardening of their hearts was the beginning of their doom. (See Deut. ii. 30.) Compare this verse with ver. 15.

VER. 21. *At that time.* That is, in the "long time" of ver. 18, perhaps during the first seven years after the *eisodus*.

Anakims. The Anakim were a strong and war-like race, one branch of which, represented by three families (Sheshai, Ahiman, and Talmai), dwelt in Hebron and the neighboring towns. From one of their ancestors, Arba, Hebron received the name of Kirjath-arba, or city of Arba (chap. xiv. 15, xv. 13, 14). The Anakim were giants (Num. xiii. 33), like the Rephaim,* Zuzim, Emim, and Horim, east of Jordan. Those east of the Jordan had been destroyed by various nations, Og, king of Bashan, having been one of the last of them (Deut. iii. 11), at least of the Rephaim. The Avim, who formerly dwelt in the Philistine country, and were destroyed by the Philistines (Deut. ii. 23), were, probably, also members of this gigantic race. We can only conjecture where, in ethnology, to put this race. They may have been a Cushite or a Turanian people, for different theories would make these two races to have spread themselves very early over the earth.

Hebron. (See on chap. x. 3.)

Debir. (See on chap. x. 38.)

Anab is ten miles south of Hebron.

The mountains of Judah; the mountains of Israel. The distinction made in the same range by the division of the land among the Israelitish tribes. Long before the division of the people by the two kingdoms in the time of Rehoboam, we find Judah and Israel distinguished. (See 1 Sam. xi. 8, and 2 Sam. xxiv. 9.) This distinction probably began at the first settlement, Judah having received the south portion of the land in general, out of which Simeon and Dan were to take their portions afterwards, while the rest of Israel had not received their parts.

* The name *Rephaim,* translated "giants," is used sometimes generically for all these races (Deut. ii. 11, 20).

22 There was none of the Anakims left in the land
of the children of Israel: only in Gaza, in Gath, and in
Ashdod, there remained.

23 So Joshua took the whole land, according to all
that the LŎRD said unto Moses, and Joshua gave it for
an inheritance unto Israel according to their divisions
by their tribes. And the land rested from war.

VER. 22. *Gaza, Gath, Ashdod.* Three of the
Philistine cities. *Gaza* and *Ashdod* are well known,
bearing still their old names, lying on the coast.
Gath is probably the present Tell es-Safieh, ten
miles east of Ashdod. Goliath, who was of Gath,
was perhaps one of this race of Anakim.

VER. 23. *And Joshua gave it for an inheritance
unto Israel according to their divisions by their
tribes.* The details are given afterwards. This
is only a proleptical statement, to close the record
of the conquest.

And the land rested from war. There were local
collisions, but no general state of war. Special
attacks were made on those cities and strongholds,
which the Israelites had, through a lack of faith,
failed to conquer at the first; and these desultory
conflicts appear to have lasted many years, until
after Joshua's death. Indeed, we find the Jebusites in Jerusalem attacked and defeated by Israel
only in David's day (2 Sam. v. 7), four hundred
years later.

CHAPTER XII.

1 Now these *are* the kings of the land, which the children of Israel smote, and possessed their land on the other side Jordan toward the rising of the sun, from the river Arnon, unto mount Hermon, and all the plain on the east:

2 Sihon king of the Amorites, who dwelt in Heshbon, *and* ruled from Aroer, which *is* upon the bank of the river Arnon, and from the middle of the river, and from half Gilead, even unto the river Jabbok, *which is* the border of the children of Ammon;

8. *Recapitulation.*

VER. 1. *The river Arnon* is the present Mojib, flowing northward on the east of Moab (Judg. xi. 18), and then abruptly turning westward near Aroer, and entering the Dead Sea about half-way between its two extremities. It flows through a deep gorge nearly two miles wide, having very steep sides or banks. This was Moab's northern boundary, and hence Israel's southern boundary, on the east of the Jordan.

Mount Hermon is the southern terminus of the Anti-Lebanon range, and the highest summit of the range, being about ten thousand feet in height. It is visible with its snowy crest over a large part of Palestine. It was the northern boundary of Israel on the east of the Jordan.

VER. 2. *Aroer*, a city on the north cliff of the

3 And from the plain to the sea of Cinneroth on the east, and unto the sea of the plain, *even* the salt sea on the east, the way to Beth-jeshimoth; and from the south, under Ashdoth-pisgah:

Arnon gorge, still retaining the old name in its ruins.

From the middle of the river. (The "from" should be omitted.) This seems to be a reduced phrase from "the city that is in the midst of the river" (chap. xiii. 9, 16), and probably refers to a portion of Aroer, or a dependent city (Ar of Moab, Num. xxi. 15, Isa. xv. 1) closely connected with Aroer, at the fork of the Mojib and its main branch, the Lejum or Enkeileh, three miles from the present ruins of Aroer. It was thus between the two parts of the river, and marked the north-eastern corner of Moab.

And from half Gilead. Rather, *even half Gilead.* Sihon ruled over half the Gilead country to the river (or torrent) Jabbok, the present Wady Zerka. Gilead is the high land between Moab and the Sea of Galilee.

Ver. 3. *And from the plain to the sea of Chinneroth on the east.* Rather, *and the Arabah to the sea of Chinneroth* (Gennesaret) *eastward* (of Jordan). Sihon ruled over the Arabah (the Jordan valley) to the sea of Chinneroth and to the sea of the Arabah, the Salt Sea, eastward of Jordan.

The way to Beth-jeshimoth, &c. This qualifies the last expression. It might be roughly rendered "Beth-jeshimothwards." That is, the Jordan

4 ¶ And the coast of Og king of Bashan, *which was*
of the remnant of the giants, that dwelt at Ashtaroth
and at Edrei,

valley extended on its western side (in Sihon's
possession) to the Salt Sea, Beth-jeshimoth being
probably at or near the junction of the Jordan and
the sea, and *southward* (not "from the south")
around the east corner of the sea to a spot under
Ashdoth-pisgah.

Ashdoth-pisgah means "the pourings-out of
Pisgah;" that is, the torrents which flow down
from the Mount Pisgah on the eastern side of the
Dead Sea, the present Wadys Ghadeimeh, Burr-
hougat, and Ghuweir. The plain extends around
the north-east corner of the sea, so as to include a
strip of land under these gorges. The word *Ash-
doth* is used in chap. xii. 40, and in ver. 8 of this
chapter, for the ravines which come down from the
mountain country of Judah to the Shephelah or
Philistine plain, and is translated in our version
"springs."

Ver. 4. *Ashtaroth*, called "Ashteroth-Karnaim"
in Gen. xiv. 5 (if, indeed, it be the same place), is
a few miles west of the Lejah, in the latitude of
Lake Semechonitis, and about thirty-five miles east
of that water. Some think, and with reason, that
this spot (now called Sunamein) is Ashteroth-
Karnaim, and that the Ashtaroth of this text is at
Afineh, on the cliffs of Jebel Hauran, and about ten
miles north-west of Salcah.

Edrei is at the south-west angle of the Lejah.

5 And reigned in mount Hermon, and in Salcah, and in all Bashan, unto the border of the Geshurites, and the Maachathites, and half Gilead, the border of Sihon king of Heshbon.

6 Them did Moses the servant of the LORD, and the children of Israel smite: and Moses the servant of the LORD gave it *for* a possession unto the Reubenites, and the Gadites, and the half-tribe of Manasseh.

7 ¶ And these *are* the kings of the country which Joshua and the children of Israel smote on this side Jordan on the west, from Baal-gad in the valley of Lebanon, even unto the mount Halak that goeth up to Seir; which Joshua gave unto the tribes of Israel *for* a possession according to their divisions;

8 In the mountains, and in the valleys, and in the plains, and in the springs, and in the wilderness, and

VER. 5. *Mount Hermon.* (See on ver 1.) *Salcah,* now Sulkhad, is at the southern edge of Jebel Hauran, occupying a most imposing site. It is on the same line of latitude with Beth-shean, and about seventy miles to the east of that place.

Bashan included all the country lying between the Jordan valley and the eastern desert, north of the Hieromax and south of Hermon.

The *Geshurites* probably occupied the region between the Lejah and Damascus.

The *Maachathites* were, no doubt, intimately connected with the Geshurites, and perhaps jointly occupied the same territory. It is curious to notice that David's wife, who was mother to Absalom, was *Maachah,* the daughter of the *Geshurite* king.

Half Gilead, i.e., the northern half, between the Jabbok (Zerka) and the Hieromax (Yarmuk).

VER. 7. See on chap. xi. 17.

VER. 8. Note the exact enumeration. 1. The

6

in the south country; the Hittites, the Amorites, and the Canaanites, the Perizzites, the Hivites, and the Jebusites:

9 ¶ The king of Jericho, one; the king of Ai, which *is* beside Beth-el, one;

10 The king of Jerusalem, one; the king of Hebron, one;

11 The king of Jarmuth, one; the king of Lachish, one;

12 The king of Eglon, one; the king of Gezer, one;

13 The king of Debir, one; the king of Geder, one;

14 The king of Hormah, one; the king of Arad, one;

15 The king of Libnah, one; the king of Adullam, one;

16 The king of Makkedah, one; the king of Beth-el, one;

17 The king of Tappuah, one; the king of Hepher, one;

18 The king of Aphek, one; the king of Lasharon, one;

19 The king of Madon, one; the king of Hazor, one;

20 The king of Shimron-meron, one ; the king of Achshaph, one;

21 The king of Taanach, one; the king of Megiddo, one;

22 The king of Kedesh, one; the king of Jokneam of Carmel, one;

23 The king of Dor in the coast of Dor, one; the king of the nations of Gilgal, one;

24 The king of Tirzah, one: all the kings thirty and one.

mountain country; 2. The Shephelah; 3. The Arabah; 4. The intervening ravine-country; 5. The wilderness (on the west side of the Dead Sea, and corresponding to No. 4); 6. The Negeb. Note also the omission of the Girgashites, as in chap. xi. 3.

VER. 9–24. The kings in this list not specially named before are those of Geder, Hormah, Arad, Adullam, Bethel, Tappuah, Hepher, Aphek, Lasharon, Taanach, Megiddo, Kedesh, Jokneam, Dor, Goim (nations), and Tirzah.*

Geder, probably the " Gedor " of Judah (chap. xv. 58), now Jedur, half-way between Hebron and Bethlehem.

Hormah (or Zephath, as in Judg. i. 17) is identified with es-Sufah by Robinson. Es-Sufah is a pass up the high mountain buttress of southern Judah, north of the remarkable Wady Fikreh. Others put Hormah at Sepata, south of Elusa.

Arad is twenty miles south of Hebron.

Adullam, supposed to be Deir Duffan, twenty-two miles south-west of Jerusalem.

Bethel, now Beitin, in close proximity to Ai (see chap. viii. 17), ten miles north of Jerusalem.

Tappuah was on the boundary between Ephraim and Manasseh (chap. xvi. 8, xvii. 8), and may be looked for not far from Ebal and Gerizim to the north-east.

Hepher, probably the same as Gath-hepher (2 Ki. xiv. 25), now el-Meshhad, between Nazareth and Sepphoris.

Aphek. There was an Aphek near Jerusalem, to the north-west (1 Sam. iv. 1). The position of the name in this list might lead us to look for this one near the plain of Esdraelon. There may have been another Aphek there, as we know there was

---

* Keil's argument to prove that the towns mentioned in verses 17 and 18 belong to the number of those conquered with the southern confederacy, and therefore are to be sought for to the south of Ai and Bethel, is plausible, but by no means conclusive.

one east of the Sea of Galilee (1 Ki. xx. 26), and another in Asher (Josh. xix. 30). Perhaps the one in Asher is here intended, and it may be identical with Haifa on the bay of Akka.

Lasharon cannot be identified, but Knobel suggests Saruneh, near the Sea of Galilee.

Taanach and *Megiddo* are well-known sites in the south-western corner of the great plain of Esdraelon.

Kedesh, afterward in the tribe of Issachar (1 Chron. vi. 72), and called " Kishon " (Josh. xxi. 28), was no doubt also in the great plain by the river Kishon.

Jokneam is found at el-Kaimon, under the southern end of Carmel.

Dor. (See on chap. xi. 2.)

Goim. The expression in the English version is " king of the nations of Gilgal," but the prefix to " Gilgal " is the same as that before " Carmel " in ver. 22, and before " the coast " in ver. 23. Hence we read " the king of Goim (nations) by Gilgal." The Goim lived near Gilgal, and were probably a mixed people having a king of their own. The Gilgal would be the Jiljilia, near Antipatris.

Tirzah is probably Telluzah, at the north of Mount Ebal. It was afterward a royal Israelitish city (1 Ki. xvi. 17).

These thirty-one kings doubtless divided the whole territory east of the Jordan from Hermon to Kadesh among them, excepting the Gibeonitish confederacy.

CHAPTER XIII.

VII. THE INHERITANCE OF THE TWO TRIBES AND A
HALF.

1 Now Joshua was old *and* stricken in years; and
the LORD said unto him, Thou art old *and* stricken in
years, and there remaineth yet very much land to be
possessed.

VER. 1. *Was old and stricken in years.* (See Gen.
xxiv. 1.) This is not a tautology. Joshua was
old not only as compared with childhood, but as
viewed with reference to the whole career of man.
Stricken is the old English for *advanced.* Joshua
was eighty-seven when he had reduced the whole
land (chap. xi. 23); that is, when he had destroyed
its opposition and possessed it generally, abolishing
its kingdoms from Kadesh to Mount Hermon.
Moses was one hundred and twenty years old
when he died, Joshua was one hundred and ten
years old when he died, and Caleb probably had
an equally long life, as he was about equal in age
with Joshua, and survived him. These three prominent men may have had their lives specially prolonged, but even if we count one hundred and ten
as the average length of life in Joshua's day,
eighty-seven would be nearly four-fifths of the
whole time, and a man of eighty-seven would be

advanced in years. However, from Moses' psalm
(Ps. xc. 10), it would appear that human life then
already had the same limits as now, and hence that
eighty-seven was an extreme old age, far beyond
the average years of man, exactly as it is to-day.

*There remaineth yet very much land to be pos-
sessed.* God had announced to Israel at Sinai
(Ex. xxiii. 29, 30) that he would not drive out
the Canaanites in one year, but by little and little,
so that the desolated land should not be filled with
wild beasts. Yet God again said (Deut. ix. 3),
through Moses, that the children of Israel should
drive them out and destroy them *quickly.* This
latter is a command, and with it can be quoted the
threat against disobedience given in Num. xxxiii.
55, and repeated by Joshua (chap. xxiii. 13), "but
if ye will not drive out the inhabitants of the land
from before you, then it shall come to pass that those
which ye let remain of them shall be pricks in
your eyes and thorns in your sides, and shall vex you
in the land wherein ye dwell." From these passages,
and from the fact that Joshua just before his death
(chap. xxiii. 14) found no fault with Israel for
leaving any of the Canaanites in the land, we
gather that at the end of the seven years' conquest
God wished Israel to cease from war (chap. xi. 23),
and did not desire a renewal of the work of extermination until after Joshua's death. The people
had already driven out the Canaanites *quickly,*
although not totally ; and now, with regard to those
left in the land, when the campaigns should com-

2 This *is* the land that yet remaineth: all the borders
of the Philistines, and all Geshuri,

mence against them, the people of Israel were to
act with like speed and faith. In the sequel we
find that they did *not* so act, and hence fell into the
evils predicted. In the twenty-three years from
the end of Joshua's conquest till his death, the
land was peacefully possessed by Israel, and the
people became numerous enough to fill up the desolated regions. (See Ex. xxiii. 29.) It will be
noticed in this order of God to Joshua (the first
seven verses of this chapter), although God says
there is very much land yet to be possessed, and
describes it, he does not command Joshua to seize
it and subdue it, but only to divide it (ver. 6, 7),
or allot it to the tribes.

VER. 2. *The Philistines*, who, with the Caphtorim, originally came out from Caphtor (probably
the Nile delta), settled in the Shephelah, or fertile
and extensive plain lying between the mountains
of Judah and the sea. (See Gen. x. 14; Deut. ii.
23; Jer. xlvii. 4; Am. ix. 7.) Their five principal
cities, Gaza, Ashdod, Ashkelon, Gath, and Ekron,
occupied advantageous points on this plain.

Gaza (now Ghuzzeh) is situated two miles from
the sea in lat. 31° 30', and has always been a place
of importance.

Ashdod, which seems to have been the religious
capital of the Philistines, as Gaza was their chief
political city, is also two miles from the sea, and
twenty-two miles north of Gaza.

3 From Sihor, which *is* before Egypt, even unto the
borders of Ekron northward, *which* is counted to the
Canaanite: five lords of the Philistines ; the Gaza-
thites, and the Ashdothites, the Eshkalonites, the
Gittites, and the Ekronites ; also the Avites :

Ashkelon lies on a rocky ridge on the edge of the
sea between Gaza and Ashdod.

Gath was probably on the strong position of
Tell es-Safieh, ten miles east of Ashdod. The hill
is two hundred feet high.

Ekron (now Akir) is nine miles from the sea,
eleven miles north of (our supposed) Gath, and
about the same distance from Ashdod, while from
Gaza to Ekron, the two most widely separated of
the Philistine cities, is a distance of thirty-three
miles. The whole land of the Philistines may be
reckoned as fifty miles in length from south to
north, and fifteen miles in breadth from the sea to
the mountains. Its southern and northern limits
would be the Wady Ghuzzeh and the southern
branch of the Nahr el-Aujeh. So large and rich a
plain could readily support a million people, and
if the advantages of the sea are added, a much
larger population could dwell there.

Geshuri, or the Geshurites, were a part of the
original inhabitants of the desert north of el-Arish
and south of Gaza (1 Sam. xxvii. 8). They were
probably Bedawin like the Amalekites and Ger-
izites (called Gezrites in l. c.), and part of their
tribe or race seem to have settled in Bashan. (See
chap. xii. 5, and in this chap. ver. 13.)

VER. 3. *Sihor* is the Nile. The words, "which

4 From the south all the land of the Canaanites, and Mearah that *is* beside the Sidonians, unto Aphek to the borders of the Amorites:

is before Egypt," would indicate the Pelusiac arm as the boundary of Egypt, to which the Israelitish possession was to extend. In David's day (1 Chron. xiii. 5), this possession was made good.

To the Canaanite. The Philistines were not Canaanites, but their land was counted as part of the Canaanitish territory.

Gittites, i.e., inhabitants of Gath.

The Avites, or Avim (Deut. ii. 23), were the old inhabitants near Gaza (Azzah in Deut. ii. 23), probably a gigantic race, who were destroyed by the Caphtorim (see on ver. 2), and a remnant of whom still dwelt among the Philistines.

VER. 4. *From the south.* Rather, *on the south.* This phrase belongs to the preceding words, thus, *Also the Avites on the south.*

The land of the Canaanites was the strip of coast land running up from Carmel to Tyre.

Mearah seems to be the designation of the Lebanon region about the Nahr ed-Damur, the Nahr Beirut and the Nahr el-Kelb. Keil's notion that it was Mugr Jezzin is too restricted.

Beside the Sidonians. Rather, *belonging to the Sidonians.*

Aphek (now Afka) is north of the sources of the Nahr el-Kelb and on the Nahr Ibrahim (Adonis). It was the spot where in later days the celebrated temple of Venus stood.

6* J

5 And the land of the Giblites, and all Lebanon toward the sun-rising, from Baal-gad under mount Hermon unto the entering into Hamath.

To the borders of the Amorites, that is, to the farthermost limit of the Amorites on the north.

VER. 5. *The Giblites.* Translated in 1 Kings v. 18, "stone-squarers" wrongly. They are the people of Gebal (Ps. lxxxiii. 7, and Ez. xxvii. 9), now Jebeil, on the coast a little north of the mouth of the Nahr Ibrahim.

All Lebanon toward the sun-rising, *i.e.*, all Lebanon lying eastward of Jebeil from Baal-gad (chap. xi. 17) to the entering into Hamath.

Unto the entering into Hamath. Or, " until one comes into Hamath." Hamath was a kingdom embracing all the course of the Orontes. Its southern limit was not far north of Baalbek, east of Aphek and Jebeil. The northern boundary of Israel is thus put along a line extending from the Mediterranean at or near Jebeil to the Bukaa, or Coele-Syria, and down the Leontes. We may imagine the Nahr Kadisha taking the line to the Lebanon pass near Bezun, and thence the Leontes forming the boundary to Jebel ed-Dahar, where the Jordan (Nahr Hasbeiya) would continue it until the neighborhood of Baneas is reached. The land in in its full dimensions would be two hundred and twenty miles long, and, starting from an apex above Jebeil, would reach a width of eighty miles at its greatest breadth, excepting the desert part between the Nile and the Arabah, which would

6 All the inhabitants of the hill-*country* from Lebanon unto Misrephoth-maim, *and* all the Sidonians, them will I drive out from before the children of Israel: only divide thou it by lot unto the Israelites for an inheritance, as I have commanded thee.

7 Now therefore divide this land for an inheritance unto the nine tribes, and the half-tribe of Manasseh.

8 With whom the Reubenites and the Gadites have received their inheritance, which Moses gave them, beyond Jordan eastward, *even* as Moses the servant of the Lord gave them;

be still more. From the most northern portion of this tract, the region of Lebanon, the old population were never dislodged, but in David's and Solomon's day it was all subject to Israel.*

VER. 7. With this verse ends God's command, which was probably given to Joshua through the instrumentality of the Urim and Thummim of the high-priest.

VER. 8. Here begins the statement of the sacred writer.

With whom. Or, " with it," *i.e.*, with the half-tribe of Manasseh, and yet not the same half of the tribe referred to in ver. 7.

As Moses the servant of the Lord gave them.

* I have in these last two verses given the received view of Israel's northern frontier, extending it fifty miles north of the mouth of the Leontes. And yet I cannot heartily accept this view. It would make Asher's portion out of all proportion with the rest (chap. xix. 24–31), and it would present a long reach of territory which Israel never pretended to claim, except by such conquest as it claimed the Euphrates on one hand, and Eziongaber on the other. The line of Hermon and the Leontes appears to be much more reasonable. In such case, of course, we should give a different account of Mearah, Aphek, and the Giblites.

9 From Aroer that *is* upon the bank of the river Arnon, and the city that *is* in the midst of the river, and all the plain of Medeba unto Dibon;

10 And all the cities of Sihon king of the Amorites, which reigned in Heshbon, unto the border of the children of Ammon;

11 And Gilead, and the border of the Geshurites and Maachathites, and all mount Hermon, and all Bashan unto Salcah ;

12 All the kingdom of Og in Bashan, which reigned in Ashtaroth and in Edrei, who remained of the remnant of the giants. For these did Moses smite, and cast them out.

13 Nevertheless, the children of Israel expelled not the Geshurites, nor the Maachathites: but the Geshurites and the Maachathites dwell among the Israelites until this day.

14 Only unto the tribe of Levi he gave none inheritance; the sacrifices of the LORD God of Israel made by fire *are* their inheritance, as he said unto them.

The repetition is to show that Moses acted by divine command.

VER. 9. *Aroer*, &c. (See on chap. xii. 2.)

The plain of Medeba unto Dibon. The same as " the field of Moab " in Num. xxi. 20, the high plateau which stretches from the Arnon to Heshbon twenty-five miles, in which is the city Medeba. *Dibon* (famous for the late discovery of " the Moabite stone ") is near its southern boundary.

VER. 10. *The children of Ammon* had been driven from the country north of the Arnon (along with the Moabites) by Sihon the Amorite (Num. xxi. 26 ; Judg. xi. 13), and were now occupying the desert on the east.

VER. 11–13. See on chap. xii. 4, 5.

VER. 14. *The tribe of Levi.* (See Num. xviii. 20–24.) While the Levites had no territory to

15 ¶ And Moses gave unto the tribe of the children of Reuben *inheritance* according to their families.

16 And their coast was from Aroer that *is* on the bank of the river Arnon, and the city that *is* in the midst of the river, and all the plain by Medeba:

17 Heshbon, and all her cities that *are* in the plain; Dibon, and Bamoth-baal, and Beth-baal-meon,

18 And Jahaza, and Kedemoth, and Mephaath,

19 And Kirjathaim, and Sibmah, and Zareth-shahar in the mount of the valley,

20 And Beth-peor, and Ashdoth-pisgah, and Beth-jeshimoth,

21 And all the cities of the plain, and all the kingdom of Sihon king of the Amorites which reigned in Heshbon, whom Moses smote with the princes of Midian, Evi and Rekem, and Zur, and Hur, and Reba, *which were* dukes of Sihon, dwelling in the country.

cultivate, they had cities to dwell in (chap. xiv. 4) as their own.

VER. 15–21. Reuben's inheritance. The Arnon (Wady el-Mojib) was its southern boundary, dividing it from Moab.

Heshbon lies twenty-five miles north of the Arnon, and fifteen miles east of the northern end of the Dead Sea.

Dibon is three miles from the Arnon.

Bamoth-baal ("Bamoth" in Num. xxi. 19), *Jahaza* or Jahaz, *Kedemoth, Mephaath, Sibmah,* and *Zareth-shahar* are not identified, though Seetzen suggests Sara near the mouth of the Zerka Main for the last.

Beth-baal-meon is ten miles south of Heshbon.

Kirjathaim is by Porter placed at Kurciyat, seven miles south of Beth-baal-meon.

Beth-peor, we know, was near Israel's encampment opposite Jericho (Deut. iii. 29, and iv. 46).

22 ¶ Balaam also the son of Beor, the sooth-sayer, did the children of Israel slay with the sword, among them that were slain by them.

23 And the border of the children of Reuben was Jordan, and the border *thereof.* This *was* the inheritance of the children of Reuben, after their families, the cities and the villages thereof.

24 And Moses gave *inheritance* unto the tribe of Gad, *even* unto the children of Gad according to their families.

25 And their coast was Jazer, and all the cities of Gilead, and half the land of the children of Ammon, unto Aroer that *is* before Rabbah;

26 And from Heshbon unto Ramath-mizpeh, and Betonim ; and from Mahanaim unto the border of Debir;

27 And in the valley, Beth-aram, and Beth-nimrah, and Succoth, and Zaphon, the rest of the kingdom of Sihon king of Heshbon, Jordan and *his* border, *even* unto the edge of the sea of Cinneroth, on the other side Jordan eastward.

28 This *is* the inheritance of the children of Gad after their families, the cities, and their villages.

For *Ashdoth-pisgah* and *Beth-jeshimoth,* see on chap. xii. 3.

With the princes of Midian (Num. xxxi. 8).

VER. 22. *Soothsayer* or "diviner." The word is used of those who pretend to be prophets.

VER. 24–28. Gad's inheritance. The south line of Gad touched Heshbon (ver. 26), and the north line touched the Sea of Galilee in the Jordan valley and Mahanaim, near the sources of Wady Yabis by the eastern plain, while the Gilead mountain-country between belonged to Manasseh ("half Gilead," ver. 31). The Jabbok was there its northern boundary. Of the ten towns mentioned, *Ramath-mizpeh* is generally identified with es-Salt, twenty miles north of Heshbon (but see on chap. xx. 8), and *Mahanaim* is placed by some at Maneh, thirty miles farther north, and twenty-five miles south-east of the Sea of Galilee.

Beth-aram and *Beth-nimrah* are both identified in the valley opposite Jericho. *Succoth*, mentioned in Jacob's history (Gen. xxxiii. 17), must be in the Jordan valley, near Wady Yabis, and not on the west side of the Jordan, as many put it. *Betonim* is near Ramath-mizpeh. *Lidbir* is supposed by Reland to be the Lodebar of 2 Sam. xvii. 27, near Mahanaim. *Jazer, Aroer,* and *Zaphon* cannot be identified.

Jazer and all the cities of Gilead (i.e., the southern half of Gilead), *even half the land of the children of Ammon* (the tribe of Reuben having the other half), *unto Aroer that is before Rabbah.* This describes the bulk of Gad's possession, Aroer marking its eastern limit. *From Heshbon unto Ramath-mizpeh, and Betonim,* expresses the length of this tract from south to north.

From Mahanaim unto the border of Lidbir (by mistake written " Debir "). This describes the eastern horn of Gad that ran north into Manasseh. Ver. 27 describes the Jordan valley and the western horn running up to the Sea of Galilee.

Reuben's tract was only twenty-five miles long, while Gad's was in parts nearly sixty miles. Yet in Num. ii. 11, 15, we find that Reuben outnumbered Gad. The difference was probably made up in the superior fertility of Reuben's land.

29 ¶ And Moses gave *inheritance* unto the half-tribe of Manasseh : and *this* was *the possession* of the half-tribe of the children of Manasseh by their families.

30 And their coast was from Mahanaim, all Bashan, all the kingdom of Og king of Bashan, and all the towns of Jair, which *are* in Bashan, threescore cities:

31 And half Gilead, and Ashtaroth, and Edrei, cities of the kingdom of Og in Bashan, *were pertaining* unto the children of Machir the son of Manasseh, *even* to the one half of the children of Machir by their families.

32 These *are the countries* which Moses did distribute for inheritance in the plains of Moab, on the other side Jordan by Jericho eastward.

33 But unto the tribe of Levi, Moses gave not *any* inheritance: the LORD God of Israel *was* their inheritance, as he said unto them.

VER. 30. The half-tribe of Manasseh had all north of the latitude of 32° 30′ (at Mahanaim), taking in all Og's great kingdom of Bashan, which extended eastward at least seventy-five miles from the Jordan, including the Hauran mountain and the Lejah (Argob or Trachouitis). Besides this, the half-tribe of Manasseh had the Gilead heights down to the Jabbok (half Gilead), in which were the towns of Jair ("Havoth-Jair," Num. xxxii. 41). Ashtaroth and Edrei (see on chap. xii. 4) are mentioned as the principal cities of this large region.

VER. 31. *Machir.* Machir was the eldest son of Manasseh, and his family became the most powerful in the tribe, almost a tribe in itself, called Machirites in Num. xxvi. 29. They probably far outnumbered the rest of the tribe, and hence this whole eastern share of Manasseh went to but a half of the Machirites. Indeed, if we examine chap. xvii., it would seem as if the Machirites were the only descendants that Manasseh had.

VER. 33. *The Lord God of Israel was their inheritance.* This was Levi's high distinction. It is, therefore, again repeated. (Comp. ver. 14, also chap. xviii. 7.) To them were the priesthood, the sacrifices, cities to dwell in, and the suburbs for their cattle (chap. xiv. 4). God exalts his service above all land-possession.

CHAPTER XIV.

VIII. The Inheritance of the Nine Tribes and a
Half. (Chap. xiv.–xix.)

1 And these *are the countries* which the children of
Israel inherited in the land of Canaan, which Eleazar
the priest, and Joshua the son of Nun, and the heads
of the fathers of the tribes of the children of Israel dis-
tributed for inheritance to them.

2 By lot *was* their inheritance, as the Lord commanded by the hand of Moses, for the nine tribes, and
for the half-tribe.

This section extends through chap. xix. The
first five verses of this chapter form the preface to
the section.

Ver. 1. *Eleazar* is here first mentioned in the
book of Joshua. His solemn investment with the
office of the high-priesthood (as the oldest living
son of Aaron) is recorded in Num. xx. 28.

Heads of the fathers of the tribes, *i.e.*, chief fathers of the tribes, one for each of the ten tribes to
be represented, Reuben and Gad being excluded,
as having their inheritance on the east side of
Jordan already assigned. These chiefs of the
tribes were designated by God to Moses, before
Israel crossed Jordan. Their names are given in
Num. xxxiv. 19–28. Caleb was one of them, representing the tribe of Judah.

3 For Moses had given the inheritance of two tribes and an half-tribe on the other side Jordan: but unto the Levites he gave none inheritance among them.

4 For the children of Joseph were two tribes, Manasseh and Ephraim: therefore they gave no part unto the Levites in the land, save cities to dwell *in*, with their suburbs for their cattle, and for their substance.

5 As the LORD commanded Moses, so the children of Israel did, and they divided the land.

6 ¶ Then the children of Judah came unto Joshua in Gilgal : and Caleb the son of Jephunneh the Kenezite said unto him, Thou knowest the thing that the LORD said unto Moses the man of God concerning me and thee in Kadesh-barnea.

VER. 3. *Among them, i.e.,* among all the tribes, not only the two and a half.

But unto the Levites. " But " should be " and."

VER. 4. *For the children of Joseph.* The " for " is used as showing how, with Levi left out, there could be so many tribes. (Comp. Gen. xlviii. 5.)

Therefore is not in the Hebrew, and should be changed to " and."

VER. 6. *Then the children of Judah,* &c. Caleb's portion is first given, as having probably been assigned him before the formal division, and as soon as " the land had rest from war." Hence that phrase is found in ver. 15. This portion was allotted to Caleb on the endorsement of the tribe of Judah.

Gilgal. The Gilgal in the centre of the land. (See on chap. ix. 6. Contrasted with Shiloh in chap. xviii. 1.)

Caleb the son of Jephunneh the Kenezite. Lord Hervey thinks that Caleb was a foreigner, a proselyte, incorporated into the tribe of Judah, one of perhaps many who by proselytism swelled the numbers of Israel. He mentions Jethro, Rahab, Ruth, and Naaman as samples. His reason for this supposition is, first, from the obscure genealogy of Caleb in the Chronicles; secondly, from the fourteenth verse of this chapter and the thirteenth verse of the next; to wit, " Hebron became the inheritance of Caleb the son of Jephunneh the *Kenezite* unto this day, because that he wholly followed Jehovah *God of Israel.*" " Unto Caleb the son of Jephunneh he gave a part *among the children of Judah.*" The words in italics would scarcely have been used of a Hebrew. His third argument is from the Edomitish names mentioned in connection with Caleb here and in the Chronicles; namely, *Kenaz* (Gen. xxxvi. 11, 15), *Shobal, Manahath* (Gen. xxxvi. 20–23), *Korah, Ithran, Elah,* and *Jephunneh,* as compared with Pinon (Gen. xxxvi. 16, 26, 41). This view of Lord Hervey has great probability. Caleb may have married into the family of Hezron, and his wife may have been a daughter of Hur (1 Chron. ii. 50). In this case, Jephunneh would be his Edomite father, and " the Kenezite " would be the Edomitish tribal appellation. Caleb's noble conduct in urging the people to go up and conquer the land on the return of the spies (Num. xiii. 30), for which he (and Joshua, who was heart and soul with him at the time) was nearly stoned by the enraged people (Num. xiv. 10), made him the object of special praise and reward from God (Num. xiv. 24; Deut. i. 36). Caleb, in this chapter, is represented as preferring his claim to this promised reward.

7 Forty years old *was* I when Moses the servant of the LORD sent me from Kadesh-barnea to espy out the land; and I brought him word again as *it was* in mine heart.

8 Nevertheless, my brethren that went up with me made the heart of the people melt : but I wholly followed the LORD my God.

Kadesh-barnea, where Israel abode so long in the desert, has been placed by Robinson at el-Weibeh, on the west heights of the Arabah, south of Wady Fikrah, but it is more likely to be at the south of the mountain region of the Azazimeh, perhaps at the wells of Mayein, although the south-east corner of Mukhrah would suit the demands of the narrative better. El-Weibeh seems to me from personal inspection a very unlikely site. It is an exposed position, and not at the extreme south of what afterward constituted the borders of Israel.

VER. 7. *Forty years old.* (See Num. chap. xiii., xiv.) The spying of the land was thirty-eight years before the *eisodus*, or entrance into Canaan. Caleb was therefore seventy-eight on entering Canaan, and when he preferred his claim, at eighty-five (ver. 10), the Israelites had been seven years in the land. These seven years mark the duration of the war of conquest.

VER. 8. *My brethren*, *i.e.*, the other spies. Of course Joshua is excepted, as Caleb shows by what he says in ver. 6, " concerning me and *thee*." ·

I wholly followed the Lord. It is not immodest for a man to assert his integrity on occasions of moment. ·(Comp. Acts xxiii. 1.) Caleb here only

9 And Moses sware on that day, saying, Surely the land whereon thy feet have trodden shall be thine inheritance, and thy children's for ever ; because thou hast wholly followed the LORD my God.

10 And now, behold the LORD hath kept me alive, as he said, these forty and five years, even since the LORD spake this word unto Moses, while *the children of* Israel wandered in the wilderness: and now, lo, I *am* this day fourscore and five years old.

11 As yet I *am as* strong this day, as *I was* in the day that Moses sent me: as my strength *was* then, even so *is* my strength now, for war, both to go out, and to come in.

12 Now therefore give me this mountain, whereof

quoted the Lord's words concerning him (Num. xxxii. 12).

VER. 9. *The land whereon thy feet have trodden.* (See Deut. i. 36.) Hebron is not specified. *That* was done by Joshua.

VER. 10. *Wandered.* Lit., "walked." The false idea that Israel was *wandering about* for forty years might be corrected by the literal translation of such verbs as this. In Num. xiv. 33, the Heb. should be translated, "your children shall be shepherds in the wilderness." The word "wander" occurs legitimately only in Num. xxxii. 13, as far as Israel is concerned. The whole forty years, viewed as a whole, may be regarded as a wandering, but we should remember that the people may for many years have remained in one centre, as at Kadesh.

VER. 11. *To go out and to come in.* A proverbial phrase for full activity. (Comp. Deut. xxxi. 2; 1 Kings iii. 7.)

VER. 12. *This mountain.* That part of the

the LORD spake in that day; for thou heardest in that
day how the Anakims *were* there, and *that* the cities
were great *and* fenced: if so be the LORD *will be* with
me, then I shall be able to drive them out, as the LORD
said.

13 And Joshua blessed him, and gave unto Caleb
the son of Jephunneh, Hebron for an inheritance.

14 Hebron therefore became the inheritance of Caleb
the son of Jephunneh the Kenezite unto this day; because that he wholly followed the LORD God of Israel.

15 And the name of Hebron before *was* Kirjath-arba;
which Arba was a great man among the Anakims. And
the land had rest from war.

mountain region where the Anakim were. The
" this " points to the following description. Caleb
thus specifies Hebron and vicinity as the part of the
region trodden by his foot as a spy which he would
prefer. He was willing to be an example to the
rest of Israel in driving out the enemy who still
here and there clung to their fastnesses. He would
take the most formidable of these foes to contend
against.

The passage should read, *for thou heardest* (the
Lord) *in that day, for the Anakim are there*, &c.
Two reasons are given why he should have Hebron:
first, the Lord's promise to give him ground which
he had trodden on as a spy; and, secondly, the
presence of the gigantic enemy.

VER. 13. *Blessed him.* With a public, official
blessing before the representatives of Judah. (See
ver. 6.)

VER. 14. *Unto this day.* The book of Joshua
was, therefore, written while Caleb still lived.

VER. 15. Read, *the name of Hebron before was*

city of Arba, the great man among the Anakim.
The old name of "city of Arba," or Kirjath-
arba, clung to the place along with the name of
Hebron. After the captivity, a thousand years
after the conquest of the Anakim, Nehemiah calls
the place Kirjath-arba (Neh. xi. 25).

CHAPTER XV.

1 *THIS* then was the lot of the tribe of the children of Judah by their families; *even* to the border of Edom, the wilderness of Zin southward *was* the uttermost part of the south coast.

JUDAH and Joseph, as the two great tribes, dividing the birthright between them (1 Chron. v. 1, 2), had the land first divided between them, their general outlines being given. Afterwards the other tribes are arranged, modifying the first division. The lot probably gave only *general* indications, while the commissioners (chap. xiv. 1) made the special allotments, according to circumstances.

Judah's Lot.

VER. 1. The south boundary is made to begin at the south end of the Dead Sea. Thus the southern part of the east boundary is included in this south boundary. It is a natural and reasonable license. This verse should read, *And the lot to the tribe of the sons of Judah, to their families, was to the boundary of Edom, the desert of Zin southwards from the extremity of Teman.* Teman means " south," it is true, but as the writer has just used " Negeb " for " south," and uses it immediately

7   J

2 And their south border was from the shore of the salt sea, from the bay that looketh southward:
3 And it went out to the south side to Maaleh-acrabbim, and passed along to Zin, and ascended up on the south side unto Kadesh-barnea, and passed along to Hezron, and went up to Adar, and fetched a compass to Karkaa:

again in ver. 2, it is almost certain that here he means " Teman " for the country of Teman, which seems to have been the southern portion of Edom, perhaps from Mount Hor to the Red Sea. The boundary of Judah was, according to this passage, the boundary of Edom, along the Arabah to the point where, in the Arabah, you reach the north extremity of Teman, near Mount Hor. This point is exactly opposite Mukhrah, near which we believe Kadesh is to be sited.

VER. 2. *Bay.* Lit., " tongue." Reference is had to the shallow basin at the south of the Dead Sea, which is shut in like a bay by the remarkable projection of land from Moab.

VER. 3. *Maaleh-Acrabbim* (" Height of Scorpions ") is supposed by Robinson to be the range of chalky cliffs which abruptly terminate the Arabah, eight miles south of the Dead Sea. Over this cliff the border passed into the Zin desert (*i.e.*, the Arabah); and when it had reached its southernmost point (see on ver. 1), it turned westward, and climbed out of the Arabah up to Kadesh (chap. xiv. 6). From Kadesh the border *passed* to Hezron, then *went up* to Adar, then *turned itself* to Karkaa, then *passed* to Azmon, and *went out* to the river of Egypt,

4 *From thence* it passed toward Azmon, and went out
unto the river of Egypt; and the goings out of that
coast were at the sea: this shall be your south coast.

and so *went out* to the sea. These different verbs
may help fix the sites of these places. We may
suppose a west line to Hezron, then on a line still
going west an ascent to Adar, then a bend north-
westwards to Karkaa, then a continuation of this
line to Azmon, and then, by another turn (Num.
xxxiv. 5), to the river of Egypt. Now the "river
of Egypt," or rather "*torrent* of Egypt," is believed
to be the Wady el-Arish. If this be so (and the
presumption is very strong), then we may put Azmon a little east of Jebel Helal, and Karkaa by
Wady el-Jerur. Adar would be on the heights by
Jebel Ikhrurim, and Hezron at the south of the
Mukhrah.

Of course all this is conjecture, but founded on
the verbs used in the description. None of these
places is identified. If our conjecture be correct,
then the tribe of Judah extended forty miles
further south than the Dead Sea, and its southern
curved boundary was one hundred miles long
from the Arabah to the mouth of Wady el-Arish. (Others would have the south boundary
run through Wady Fikrah, Wady Maderah, and
Wady Muzzeh).

VER. 4. *This shall be your south coast.* This is
an insertion of the sacred writer, asserting to all
Israel that Judah's south boundary thus given
should be the south boundary of all Israel.

5 And the east border *was* the salt sea, *even* unto the end of Jordan: and *their* border in the north quarter *was* from the bay of the sea, at the uttermost part of Jordan:
6 And the border went up to Beth-hogla, and passed along by the north of Beth-arabah; and the border went up to the stone of Bohan the son of Reuben:

VER. 5. The east border of Judah (excluding the east border already given in the south border, see on ver. 1) was the Dead Sea in its entire length, the north border finding its eastern corner at the northern extremity of that sea, where the Jordan empties into it. The north border is de-scribed from this verse to ver. 11, inclusive, and although this border is not much more than half the length of the south border, yet far more details are given, on account of the greater importance of this inter-tribal border, and also on account of the well-marked localities which made an exact description easy.

VER. 6. *Beth-hogla* (now Ain-hajla) is about four miles north-west of the exit of the Jordan. The border *went up* out of the Jordan hollow to this point.

Beth-arabah must have been in the northern Arabah or Ghor, as was Beth-hogla. In ver. 61, it is said to be in "the wilderness," which name includes evidently so much of the depressed plain of Jordan as belonged to Judah. Since in chap. xviii., where this border is again given, a "shoulder" or ridge is mentioned (translated "side"), as by Beth-arabah and Beth-hogla, we may put Beth-arabah

7 And the border went up toward Debir from the valley of Achor, and so northward looking toward Gilgal, that *is* before the going up to Adummim, which *is* on the south side of the river: and the border passed toward the waters of En-shemesh, and the goings out thereof were at En-rogel:

west of Beth-hogla, about a mile near the ridge of Katar Hhadije, a low ridge running through the Arabah to the Dead Sea. (See Keil.)

The stone of Bohan the son of Reuben was some monument erected probably by Israel while encamping at Gilgal, after taking Jericho, perhaps commemorating a prominent Reubenite. It must have been on the spur of the heights west of the Ghor.

VER. 7. *The valley of Achor* must be the Wady Kelt. (See on chap. vii. 24.) Up that wady the line ran toward *Debir* (somewhere near the Khan Hudrur, near which is Wady Dabor). Then it turned northward to *Gilgal* ("Geliloth" in chap. xviii. 17), which is opposite *the going up to Adummim*. This latter place is identified with Kalaat ed-Dem on the north of the Jerusalem and Jericho road, where the soil is red. Adummim signifies "red." This Gilgal (or Geliloth), therefore, is a place near this spot, and not the Gilgal where Israel encamped down in the Arabah or Ghor.

The *river* mentioned here is Wady Kelt. The word means "torrent," or "torrent-valley."

En-shemesh is now Ain el-Hodh, below Bethany.

En-rogel is the well-known fountain of Job or Nehemiah in the deep defile south-east of Jerusalem.

8 And the border went up by the valley of the son of Hinnom, unto the south side of the Jebusite; the same *is* Jerusalem: and the border went up to the top of the mountain that *lieth* before the valley of Hinnom westward, which *is* at the end of the valley of the giants northward:

9 And the border was drawn from the top of the hill unto the fountain of the water of Nephtoah, and went out to the cities of mount Ephron; and the border was drawn to Baalah, which *is* Kirjath-jearim:

10 And the border compassed from Baalah westward unto mount Seir, and passed along unto the side of mount Jearim (which *is* Chesalon) on the north side, and went down to Beth-shemesh, and passed on to Timnah:

VER. 8. *The valley of the son of Hinnom* is the deep ravine skirting the south of Jerusalem. It is called here also "the valley of Hinnom" (*ge-hinnom*), from which form comes the use of Ge-henna for the place of eternal punishment.

The Jebusite. So "the Archite" and "the Japhletite" in the Hebrew (chap. xvi. 2, 3). The Gentile noun is used for the noun of locality.

The valley of the giants (Rephaim) is a broad and shallow depression running southward from the brow of the valley of Hinnom.

The mountain mentioned in this verse is the ridge by the Convent of the Cross.

VER. 9. *Nephtoah* is now Lifta, on the edge of Wady Beit Hanina.

Mount Ephron must be the high range from Neby Samwil to Soba.

Baalah, or *Kirjath-jearim*, is identified with Kuryet el-Enab.

VER. 10. *Mount Seir* is the high ridge on which is Saris.

11 And the border went out unto the side of Ekron northward: and the border was drawn to Shicron, and passed along to mount Baalah, and went out unto Jabneel; and the goings out of the border were at the sea.

12 And the west border *was* to the great sea, and the coast *thereof:* this *is* the coast of the children of Judah round about, according to their families.

13 ¶ And unto Caleb the son of Jephunneh he gave a part among the children of Judah, according to the commandment of the LORD to Joshua, *even* the city of Arba to the father of Anak, which *city is* Hebron.

14 And Caleb drove thence the three sons of Anak, Sheshai, and Ahiman, and Talmai, the children of Anak.

15 And he went up thence to the inhabitants of Debir: and the name of Debir before *was* Kirjath-sepher.

Mount Jearim, or *Chesalon* (on Mount Jearim), is now Kesla, on the lofty summit between Wady Ghurah and Wady Ismain.

Beth-shemesh is now Ain Shems.

Timnath, conspicuous in Samson's history, is Tibneh, where one looks out on the Philistine plain.

VER. 11. *Ekron.* (See chap. xiii. 3.)

Shicron cannot be identified.

Mount Baalah must be the ridge west of Ekron.

Jabneel is Yebna, south and west of the Nahr Rubin.

VER. 12. The west border of Judah was the Mediterranean Sea.

VER. 13. See on chap. xiv. 6–15.

VER. 14–19. This reconquest of Hebron and vicinity occurred after Joshua's death. (See Judg. i. 1, 9–15.) It is here inserted as appertaining to the history of Judah's allotment. The

16 ¶ And Caleb said, He that smiteth Kirjath-sepher, and taketh it, to him will I give Achsah my daughter to wife.

17 And Othniel the son of Kenaz, the brother of Caleb, took it: and he gave him Achsah his daughter to wife.

18 And it came to pass, as she came *unto him*, that she moved him to ask of her father a field: and she

reason why Caleb waited more than twenty years before reconquering his inheritance may have been his desire to see all others settled before himself, for he was a man of a large and noble nature.

The three sons of Anak is probably the three *families* of the Anakim.

Debir. (See on chap. x. 38.)

VER. 16. Caleb was now (*i.e.*, after Joshua's death) about one hundred and eight years old, and hence sought others to fight his battles.

VER. 17. *Othniel the son of Kenaz, the brother of Caleb.* The Masorites, by their pointing (both here and in Judg. i. 13, and iii. 9), make Othniel the brother of Caleb. This would make Achsah marry her uncle, which Keil asserts was not forbidden in the law. It seems, however, to be against the spirit of Lev. xviii. 14. Moreover, it is unlikely that Caleb should have a brother so young as to be a judge of Israel for forty years after Joshua's death (Judg. iii. 11). I prefer, therefore, to take the word " brother " to refer to Kenaz, the younger brother of Caleb, whose son was Othniel. Kenaz would be a family name, repeated in Othniel's father.

VER. 18. Achsah induced her new husband to

lighted off *her* ass; and Caleb said unto her, What
wouldest thou?
    19 Who answered, Give me a blessing; for thou
hast given me a south land, give me also springs of
water: and he gave her the upper springs, and the
nether springs.
    20 This *is* the inheritance of the tribe of the children
of Judah according to their families.

ask a piece of land from her father. This being
given, Achsah herself, on alighting from her ass at
her husband's dwelling, to which Caleb had accompanied her, *looks* a request at her father, and, on
his inquiry, *speaks* it.

Caleb had given her, as a marriage portion, at
Othniel's request, a south land (or, lit., "*the* south
land"), probably a well-known region near Hebron,
which was exposed to extreme heats. Achsah
asks for the possession of springs, to which her
cattle may have access. The father, full of affection, gives her more than she asks for. He gives
her two sources of water, known in the neighborhood as Gulloth Illiyyoth and Gulloth Tach-
tiyyoth ("the upper springs" and "the lower
springs").

VER. 20. This is the preface to the list of principal towns of Judah, which follow in four sec-
tions, those in the *Negeb* (the technical "south"
of Judah, including all south of a line from the
Dead Sea opposite el-Lisan to the Mediterranean
near Gaza), those in the *Shephelah* (the fertile
plain on the coast), those in the mountain country,
and those in the wilderness (the Jordan valley
and west skirts of the Dead Sea). In this list the

7*

21 And the uttermost cities of the tribe of the children of Judah toward the coast of Edom southward
were Kabzeel, and Eder, and Jagur,
22 And Kinah, and Dimonah, and Adadah,
23 And Kedesh, and Hazor, and Ithman,
24 Ziph, and Telem, and Bealoth,
25 And Hazor, Hadattah, and Kerioth, *and* Hezron,
which *is* Hazor,
26 Amam, and Shema, and Moladah,

absence of the conjunction shows in each case the
beginning of a new group.

VER. 21. First Division. The towns of the
Negeb. This region was intermediate between
the fertile country and the desert. It was princi-
pally a grazing country, though here and there
susceptible of cultivation.

First group. *Kabzeel, Eder,* and *Jagur* are not
identified.

VER. 22. *Kinah, Dimonah, Adadah.* All unknown.

VER. 23. *Kedesh* is Kadesh-barnea (chap. xiv.
6.) *Hazor* is probably the Hezron of chap. xv. 3.
Ithman is unknown.

VER. 24. Second group. *Ziph, Telem, Bealoth.*
All unknown.

VER. 25. Should read, " *And Hazor-hadattah*
(new Hazor), *and Kerioth-hezron, which is Hazor.*"
These places are unknown. Hazor and Hezron
each mean " walled town." Hence the name is
common.

VER. 26. Third group. *Amam* and *Shema* are
unknown. *Moladah* is el-Milh, east of Beer-
sheba.

27 And Hazar-gaddah, and Heshmon, and Beth-palet,

28 And Hazar-shual, and Beer-sheba, and Bizjothjah,

29 Baalah, and Iim, and Azem,

30 And Eltolad, and Chesil, and Hormah,

31 And Ziklag, and Madmannah, and Sansannah,

32 And Lebaoth, and Shilhim, and Ain, and Rimmon: all the cities *are* twenty and nine, with their villages:

VER. 27. *Hazar-gaddah*, *Heshmon*, *Beth-palet*, are unknown.

VER. 28. *Hazar-shual* and *Bizjothjah* are unknown. *Beer-sheba* is Bir es-Seba.

VER. 29. Fourth group. *Baalah*, *Iim*, *Azem*, are unknown.

VER. 30. *Eltolad* and *Chesil* are unknown, although Knobel ingeniously connects the latter with Khulasa (Elusa). It seems to be the same as Bethul of chap. xix. 4, Bethuel of 1 Chron. iv. 30, and Bethel of 1 Sam. xxx. 27. *Hormah*. (See on chap. xii. 14.)

VER. 31. *Ziklag* is probably Aslaj on the road from el-Milh to Abdeh. *Madmannah* and *Sansannah*, called Beth-marcabeth and Hazar-susah in chap. xix. 5, are not known.

VER. 32. *Lebaoth* is Beth-lebaoth in chap. xix. 6, and Beth-birei in 1 Chron. iv. 31. *Shilhim* is Sharuhen in chap. xix. 6, and Shaaraim in 1 Chron. iv. 31. Neither of these are known, nor are *Ain* and *Rimmon*.

Twenty and nine. There are thirty-six in the list. As numbers were always liable to incorrect transcription, this is doubtless an instance.

33 *And* in the valley, Eshtaol, and Zoreah, and Ashnah,

34 And Zanoah, and En-gannim, Tappuah, and Enam,

35 Jarmuth, and Adullam, Socoh, and Azekah,

36 And Sharaim, and Adithaim, and Gederah, and Gederothaim; fourteen cities with their villages:

37 Zenan, and Hadashah, and Migdal-gad,

38 And Dilean, and Mizpeh, and Joktheel,

VER. 33. Second Division. *In the valley, i.e.,* the Shephelah. The "Ashedoth," or "outpourings of the wadies," are included here in the Shephelah. These Ashedoth are the western spurs of the mountains. The word is translated "springs" in chap. xii. 8.

First group. *Eshtaol* is probably Yeshu'a, fourteen miles west of Jerusalem. *Zoreah* is Zurah, very near to Eshtaol. *Ashnah* is unknown.

VER. 34. *Zanoah* is Zanua. *En-gannim* is unknown.

Second group. *Tappuah* and *Enam* are unknown.

VER. 35. Third group. *Jarmuth.* (See on chap. xii. 15.) *Adullam.* (See on chap. xii. 15.)

Fourth group. *Socoh* is Shuweikeh, near to and south of Jarmuth. *Azekah.* (See on chap. x. 10.)

VER. 36. *Sharaim,* or Shaaraim, is undoubtedly Tell Zakariya on the edge of Wady Sumt. *Adithaim, Gederah,* and *Gederothaim* are unknown *Gederah* may be Kudna, south of Deir Dubban.

Fourteen cities. There are fifteen in the list. (See remark on ver. 32.)

VER. 37–41. Fifth group. *Zenan, Hadashah,*

39 Lachish, and Bozkath, and Eglon,
40 And Cabbon, and Lahmam, and Kithlish,
41 And Gederoth, Beth-dagon, and Naamah, and
Makkedah; sixteen cities with their villages:
42 Libnah, and Ether, and Ashan, ·
43 And Jiphtah, and Ashnah, and Nezib,
44 And Keilah, and Achzib, and Mareshah; nine
cities with their villages:
45 Ekron, with her towns and her villages:
46 From Ekron even unto the sea, all that *lay* near
Ashdod, with their villages:
47 Ashdod, with her towns and her villages; Gaza,
with her towns and her villages, unto the river of
Egypt, and the great sea, and the border *thereof:*

Migdal-gad, Dilean, Mizpeh, Joktheel. Sixth group.
*Lachish, Bozkath, Eglon, Cabbon, Lahmam, Kithlish,
Gederoth.* Seventh group. *Beth-dagon, Naamah,
Makkedah.* Of these sixteen towns only *Lachish*
and *Eglon* are identified with any certainty. (See
on chap. x. 3.) *Migdal-gad* may be Mejdel, near
Ashkelon, and *Cabbon* possibly may be Kubeibeh,
seven miles east of Eglon. *Gederoth* is prob-
ably the same as the Kedron of 1 Macc. xv. 39, 41,
and xvi. 9, now Kutrah, south of the Nehr Rubin.
Joktheel may be Huleikat, north of Um Lakis.
Makkedah. (See on chap. x. 10.)

VER. 42–44. Eighth group. *Libnah, Ether,
Ashan, Jiphtah, Ashnah, Nezib, Keilah, Achzib,
Mareshah.* For *Libnah,* see on chap. x. 29.
Keilah may be Kila, at the head of the Safieh or
Monsurah Wady. *Achzib* is put at Ain Kusaba
by Keil. *Mareshah* is probably Maresh, south of
Beit Jibrin. *Nezib* is Beit Nusib, near Kila. The
other four places are unknown.

VER. 45–47. Ninth group. *Ekron, Ashdod,* and

48 ¶ And in the mountains, Shamir, and Jattir, and
Socoh,
49 And Dannah, and Kirjath-sannah, which *is* Debir,
50 And Anab, and Eshtemoh, and Anim,
51 And Goshen, and Holon, and Giloh; eleven cities
with their villages:

Gaza are mentioned of the Philistine cities, because
they touch the northern, western, and southern
limits of the Philistine land.   Gath and Ashkelon
are omitted, as included in this outline.   No further
detail is given, because Israel never gained full
possession of this region until the days of Solomon,
and even then did not themselves occupy it.

Ver. 46. Read, *From Ekron seaward* (or westward), *all* (*i.e.*, the cities) *that was on the Ashdod
side and their* (the unnamed cities) *villages.* Between Ekron and Ashdod were some large and
important Philistine cities, although not so famous
as the five, as, for example, Jabneh (2 Chron.
xxvi. 6), called Jabneel in this chapter, ver. 11.
The LXX reads Jabneh (in the form Jemnai) in
this place for the phrase " even unto the sea."

Ver. 47. *The river of Egypt.* (See on ver. 4.)
The border of the great sea is the strip of land between the cities and the water.

Ver. 48. Third Division. *In the mountains, i.e.,*
in the " hill-country," or mountain centre of the region between the Dead Sea and the Mediterranean.
Its height at Hebron is three thousand feet above
the sea.   It is a limestone range, with rich valleys.

Ver. 48–51. First group. *Shamir* is unknown.
Jattir is Attir. *Socoh* is Shuweikeh. *Dannah*

52 Arab, and Dumah, and Eshean,
53 And Janum, and Beth-tappuah, and Aphekah,
54 And Humtah, and Kirjath-arba (which *is* Hebron)
and Zior; nine cities with their villages:
55 Maon, Carmel, and Ziph, and Juttah,
56 And Jezreel, and Jokdeam, and Zanoah,
57 Cain, Gibeah, and Timnah; ten cities with their
villages:

is perhaps, as Knobel suggests, Zanutah. *Kirjath-sannah*, or Debir. (See on chap. x. 38.) *Anab* is still so called. *Eshtemoh* is es-Semua. *Anim* is el-Ghuwein. *Goshen, Holon*, and *Giloh* are unknown. The first of the three is, doubtless, connected with the "land of Goshen" of chap. x. 41, and chap. xi. 16. (See l. c.) All this group occupies the region about the sources of Wady el-Khulil.

VER. 52–54. Second group. *Arab* and *Eshean* are unknown. *Dumah* is Daumeh. *Janum* and *Aphekah* are unknown. *Beth-tappuah* is Teffuh. *Humtah* and *Zior* are unknown. *Kirjath-arba*, or Hebron. (See on chap. x. 3.) All this group is north of the first.

VER. 55–56. Third group. *Maon* is Main. *Carmel* is Kurmul. These two places are so close together, that the lack of a conjunction cannot be considered as putting them in different groups. Perhaps the conjunction has dropped out. *Ziph* is Zif. *Juttah* is Jutta. *Jezreel, Jokdeam,* and *Zanoah* are unknown. This group lies east of the other two.

VER. 57. Fourth group. *Cain, Gibeah,* and *Timnah* are unknown. A *wav* (*i.e.,* "and") is probably dropped between Cain and Gibeah.

58 Halhul. Beth-zur, and Gedor,
59 And Maarath, and Beth-anoth, and Eltekon; six cities with their villages:
60 Kirjath-baal (which *is* Kirjath-jearim) and Rabbah; two cities with their villages:
61 In the wilderness, Beth-araba, Middin, and Secacah,
62 And Nibshan, and the city of Salt, and En-gedi; six cities with their villages.

VER. 58, 59. Fifth group. *Halhul, Beth-zur*, and *Gedor* still retain their names, scarcely altered at all. *Maarath* may be Beit Kheiran. *Beth-anoth* is Beit-anim. *Eltekon* is unknown. This group is north of all the preceding. The sixth group, as given in the LXX, is wanting in the Hebrew. They have been accidentally dropped out. They are Theko (Tekua), Ephratha or Baithleem (Bethlehem, now Beit-lahm), Phagor (Faghur), Aitan (Ain Attan), Koulon (Kuloniyeh), Tatam, Thobes, Karem (Ain Karim), Galem, Thether (Bittir), and Manocho. This group is north of all the rest.

VER. 60. Seventh group. *Kirjath-baal*, or Kirjath-jearim. (See on chap. ix. 17.) *Rabbah* is not identified.

VER. 61, 62. Fourth Division. *In the wilderness*, *i.e.*, the eastern slope of the mountain region, which is bare and rugged to the Dead Sea, and including so much of the Jordan plain as appertained to Judah. It was all a barren region, except in small oases by fountains.

Beth-arabah. (See on ver. 6.) *Middin* is perhaps Mird. *Secacah* may be Ain ·el-Feshkhah. *Nibshan* cannot be identified. *Ir-hammelach* (city

63 ¶ As for the Jebusites, the inhabitants of Jerusalem, the children of Judah could not drive them out: but the Jebusites dwell with the children of Judah at Jerusalem unto this day.

of salt) may be preserved in the Wady er-Rmail. It must have been in that southern region of the Dead Sea. (Comp. 2 Sam. viii. 13; 2 Ki. xiv. 7; Ps. lx. 2.) *En-gedi* is Ain Jidi.

VER. 63. *With the children of Judah.* Jerusalem belonged to Benjamin. But on comparing chap. xviii. 28, Judg. i. 21, and this verse together, it seems that Judah and Benjamin had combined to reduce this city, but on failing, had both been represented in the settlement of the lower town, the citadel on Zion remaining till David's time in the hands of the Jebusites.

K

CHAPTER XVI.

JOSEPH'S LOT.

1 AND the lot of the children of Joseph fell from Jordan by Jericho, unto the water of Jericho, on the east, to the wilderness that goeth up from Jericho throughout mount Beth-el,

VER. 1. *Fell.* Heb., "went forth." The word constantly used with this translation in all this description of boundary. "The lot went forth" means exactly the same with "the border went forth," as in verses 6 and 8, the lot being used metaphorically for its result.

The water of Jericho is the celebrated Ain es-Sultan, the source of Jericho's fertility.

On the east. This phrase is used here pregnantly. It means that this line from the Jordan to Jericho's waters was east of the Mount Bethel wilderness, and yet it serves to show that this whole portion of the boundary was the eastern portion. The "to" is not found in the Hebrew before "the wilderness."

Mount Bethel is the high bare region lying east of Bethel, on which probably the golden calf of Bethel was in later ages situated.

This boundary probably followed up the Wady Nawaimeh and Mutyah the whole way from the Jordan to Bethel.

2 And goeth out from Beth-el to Luz, and passeth along unto the borders of Archi to Ataroth,

3 And goeth down westward to the coast of Japhleti, unto the coast of Beth-horon the nether, and to Gezer: and the goings out thereof are at the sea.

4 So the children of Joseph, Manasseh and Ephraim, took their inheritance.

VER. 2. *From Bethel to Luz.* This Luz is Khurbet el-Lozeh, three and a half miles west of Bethel, which was perhaps the city built by the man who came from the other Luz (Bethel). (See Judg. i. 26. Also see Van de Velde's Notes on the Map, 2d ed. p. 16.)

The borders of Archi, or rather "the border of the Archite." The Archite, like the "Jebusite," may refer to a remnant of an old Canaanite tribe, or some inhabitant of the Babylonian Erech (of which "Archite" is the Gentile noun) may have settled in this part of Canaan.

Ataroth cannot be Atara, a mile or two south of Beeroth, but must be sought near the nether Beth-horon. (See chap. xviii. 13.)

VER. 3. *Japhleti.* Rather, "the Japhletite." Who he was we cannot tell. But his locality must have been, it seems, between Wady Suleiman and the Beth-horon pass.

Gezer. (See on chap. x. 33.)

The places mentioned in these surveys are not' necessarily *on* the lines. They may be mentioned as prominent localities *near* the lines. We believe that the line of Joseph started at the Jordan with Wady Nawaimeh, and followed that wady (afterward

5 ¶ And the border of the children of Ephraim according to their families was *thus:* even the border of their inheritance on the east side was Ataroth-addar, unto Beth-horon the upper;

6 And the border went out toward the sea to Michmethah on the north side; and the border went about eastward unto Taanath-shiloh, and passed by it on the east to Janohah;

called Mutyah) to Bethel's vicinity, and then struck over to Wady Budrus and Wady Muzeirah to the sea. This would be a natural and readily followed boundary. But in making it, we cannot consider the places mentioned as exactly on the line.

VER. 5. The border of Ephraim is here designated as forming a part of Joseph. There seems to be some error in the text in this verse. We should expect to read, " the border of their inheritance (*i.e.*, their south border) was *from* the east to Ataroth-addar and Beth-horon the *nether.*" The same boundary of course as that described in ver. 1–3 is here intended, for Ephraim lying south of Manasseh would have Joseph's south boundary as *his* south boundary. The Hebrew *mizrachah*, " on the east side," may be an error for *mimmizrach*, " from the east." Or *mizrachah* may mean, " beginning on the east side." (See remark on *yammah* in the next note.) *Ataroth-addar* must be the same as Ataroth in ver. 2. Beth-horon the nether lies at the foot of the pass on a rising ground, and by *it* swept the boundary line (ver. 3). It is true Beth-horon the upper is not far off, at the summit of the pass; but why should the change be made?

VER. 6. *Michmethah* is " over against " (al pné)

7 And it went down from Janohah to Ataroth, and
to Naarath, and came to Jericho, and went out at
Jordan.

Shechem (chap. xvii. 7). This is generally used
for an easterly direction, yet it need not be very
near, as Mount Abarim is over against Jericho, and
yet fifteen miles off. (Deut. xxxii. 49.)

The border here is evidently the north border of
Ephraim, and the description begins at the middle
and runs eastward. The difficulty is in rendering
hayyammah (" toward the sea "). We should expect "*from* the sea." It is probable that a clause
has dropped out, and that this phrase, "and the
border went out to the sea," belongs to the south
boundary and the fifth verse. Then there may
have been a sentence, " *and the border passed from
the sea* to Michmethah on the north side." Yet
" yammah" is used in chap. xviii. 15, for " on the
west," and may possibly refer here to the beginning
of the north border as on the west of what follows.
Michmethah may be at the south end of the
Mukhna, where some place the brook Mochmur of
Judith vii. 18, near Akrabeh (Ekrebel of Judith,
l. c.) In that case, *Taanath-shiloh* would be on the
Makhfuriyeh Wady, receiving its name perhaps
from its nearness to Shiloh.

Janohah is Yanun.

VER. 7. *Ataroth* (evidently a different place
from the Ataroth of ver. 2 and ver. 5) and *Naarath* are not known.

Came to Jericho. Very curiously the north and

8 The border went out from Tappuah westward unto the river Kanah; and the goings out thereof were at the sea. This *is* the inheritance of the tribe of the children of Ephraim by their families.

9 And the separate cities for the children of Ephraim *were* among the inheritance of the children of Manasseh, all the cities with their villages.

10 And they drave not out the Canaanites that dwelt in Gezer: but the Canaanites dwell among the Ephraimites unto this day, and serve under tribute.

south boundaries of Ephraim met at Jericho. From Jericho to the Jordan we must draw separate lines for the two, or else why should the Jordan be mentioned at all in the north boundary? Perhaps the south boundary was Wady Nawaimeh, and the north boundary was Wady Diab, the Jericho *district* being intended by " Jericho."

VER. 8. *Tappuah* I would put at or near Hareth on the Wady Kanah, and consider this wady the river Kanah, becoming the Nahr el-Anjeh as it approaches the sea.

VER. 9. (Comp. chap. xvii. 11.) There may have been in this intermingling of tribal territory a design to maintain the common brotherhood.

VER. 10. *Gezer* was a border town (see ver. 3), and, if the present Yasur, was on the south bank of the wady that was Ephraim's south border.

CHAPTER XVII.

1 THERE was also a lot for the tribe of Manasseh; for he *was* the first-born of Joseph; *to wit*, for Machir the first-born of Manasseh, the father of Gilead: because he was a man of war, th'erefore he had Gilead and Bashan.

2 There was also *a lot* for the rest of the children of Manasseh by their families; for the children of Abiezer, and for the children of Helek, and for the children of Asriel, and for the children of Shechem, and for the children of Hepher, and for the children of Shemida: these *were* the male children of Manasseh the son of Joseph by their families.

3 ¶ But Zelophehad, the son of Hepher, the son of Gilead, the son of Machir, the son of Manasseh, had no sons, but daughters: and these *are* the names of his daughters, Mahlah, and Noah, Hoglah, Milcah, and Tirzah.

VER. 1. Manasseh's lot is described as forming part of Joseph. For the descendants of Machir, see on chap. xiii. 31.

VER. 2. According to Num. xxvi. 29–32, these six families of Manasseh's tribe were descended also from Machir. They were, moreover, all descended from Gilead, *i.e.*, all "Gileadites" (Num. xxvi. 29). These Gileadites had shown remarkable valor in conquering the country east of Jordan, and hence had received a double inheritance, one portion on the east side, in addition to their portion on the west.

VER. 3. *Zelophehad* seems to have been the only representative of the Hepherites, or children of

4 And they came near before Eleazar the priest, and before Joshua the son of Nun, and before the princes, saying, The LORD commanded Moses to give us an inheritance among our brethren : therefore according to the commandment of the LORD he gave them an inheritance among the brethren of their father.

5 And there fell ten portions to Manasseh, besides the land of Gilead and Bashan, which *were* on the other side Jordan;

6 Because the daughters of Manasseh had an inheritance among his sons: and the rest of Manasseh's sons had the land of Gilead.

7 ¶ And the coast of Manasseh was from Asher to Michmethah, that *lieth* before Shechem; and the border went along on the right hand unto the inhabitants of En-tappuah.

8 *Now* Manasseh had the land of Tappuah: but Tappuah on the border of Manasseh *belonged* to the children of Ephraim:

Hepher. Hence his five daughters received the Hepherite portion by a special legislation. (See Num. xxvii. 1–11.)

VER. 4. They now prefer their claim.

VER. 5. *Ten portions.* Six as above; to wit, the Abiezrites, Helekites, Asrielites, Shechemites, Hepherites (represented by Zelophehad's daughters), and Shemidaites. Besides these, there must have been four other Manassite families, not Gileadites, perhaps not Machirites, represented on the west side.

VER. 7. *Asher.* Not the tribe, but a town. I take it to be Ausarin, on the Makhfuriyeh Wady. For *Michmethah* and *En-tappuah* (Tappuah), see on chap. xvi. 6, 8. For *Shechem*, see chap. xx. 7.

VER. 8. The land of Tappuah would be the Jebel Salmon or Sleiman.

9 And the coast descended unto the river Kanah, southward of the river. These cities of Ephraim *are* among the cities of Manasseh: the coast of Manasseh also *was* on the north side of the river, and the outgoings of it were at the sea:

10 Southward *it was* Ephraim's, and northward *it was* Manasseh's, and the sea is his border; and they met together in Asher on the north, and in Issachar on the east.

11 And Manasseh had in Issachar and in Asher, Beth-shean and her towns, and Ibleam and her towns, and the inhabitants of Dor and her towns, and the inhabitants of En-dor and her towns, and the inhabitants of Taanach and her towns, and the inhabitants of Megiddo and her towns, *even* three countries.

VER. 9. There must be an error in this text. I would read, " And the coast descended unto the river Kanah. Southward of the river these cities are of Ephraim, and the coast of Manasseh was on the north side of the river." Keil's explanation only makes the " muddle " worse. For the river Kanah, see on chap. xvi. 8.

VER. 10. *And they met together in Asher.* Rather, " And they (the Manassites) reached to Asher." They reached Asher on the coast, and they reached Issachar on the great plain.

Issachar on the east, i.e., on the east of Asher.

VER. 11. *Beth-shean* is Beisan. *Ibleam* is supposed to be at Jelameh. *Dor* is Tantura. *En-dor* bears the same name still on the Duhy Mountain. *Taanach* is Taanuk. *Megiddo* is Lejjun.

Three countries. Rather, " the three heights," probably the name given to the Tell Taanuk, the Tell Metsellim, and the height on which Megiddo stood. Taanach and Megiddo are twin towns, and

8

12 Yet the children of Manasseh could not drive out
the inhabitants of those cities; but the Canaanites would
dwell in that land.

13 Yet it came to pass, when the children of Israel
were waxen strong, that they put the Canaanites to
tribute; but did not utterly drive them out.

14 And the children of Joseph spake unto Joshua,
saying, Why hast thou given me *but* one lot and one
portion to inherit, seeing I *am* a great people, forasmuch
as the LORD hath blessed me hitherto?

15 And Joshua answered them, If thou *be* a great
people, *then* get thee up to the wood-*country*, and cut
down for thyself there in the land of the Perizzites
and of the giants, if mount Ephraim be too narrow for
thee.

Megiddo occupied probably the two heights indicated.

VER. 12. The fact that these towns were within
the borders of another tribe probably caused this
apathy.   See the case of Gezer in chap. xvi. 10.

VER. 13. The old " cherem " order of God was
forgotten and neglected as time passed on.

VER. 14. They call it one lot and one portion,
because the portion had probably been drawn by
one lot out of the urn.   But it was ample for the
two tribes, or rather the one tribe and a half, for
they were less numerous than other single tribes.
They forget, too, that a part of their brethren had
inherited the largest section of all beyond the Jordan.   The Ephraimites were probably the principal complainers.   Compare their conduct at other
times (Judg. viii. 1, and xii. 1).

VER. 15. Joshua gives them permission to go to
the highlands of the Perizzites and giants (Rephaim) and settle.   Those highlands are probably the

16 And the children of Joseph said, The hill is not enough for us: and all the Canaanites that dwell in the land of the valley have chariots of iron, *both they* who *are* of Beth-shean and her towns, and *they* who *are* of the valley of Jezreel.

17 And Joshua spake unto the house of Joseph, *even* to Ephraim and to Manasseh, saying, Thou *art* a great people, and hast great power: thou shalt not have one lot *only:*

18 But the mountain shall be thine; for it *is* a wood, and thou shalt cut it down: and the out-goings of it shall be thine: for thou shalt drive out the Canaanites, though they have iron chariots, *and* though they *be* strong.

mountains of Gilboa, lying between Beth-shean and Jezreel. A remnant of the Perizzites and Rephaim had strengthened themselves there.

Mount Ephraim is the mountain-land north of Judah and extending to the great plain, and lying between the coast-plain and the Jordan Ghor. It is now so called, as Ephraim had just received a part of it as an inheritance. There is some irony in Joshua's words, and he may call the region Mount Ephraim, because Ephraim was the chief complainer.

VER. 16. *The hill.* Rather, " the mountain." That is, the Gilboa mountain just offered them. That would not be enough, and they could not descend and occupy any of the Beth-shean plain east of Gilboa, or of the Jezreel plain west of Gilboa, because of the formidable chariots of the Canaanites still holding those parts.

VER. 17, 18. Joshua continues his irony. They were so strong and brave a people, that they should have another lot, the Gilboa country and its adjoining parts (outgoings), and should overcome the fierce enemies. We have no proof that Ephraim and half Manasseh ever used this permission. The love of ease and fear of their foes combined to deter them from ridding the land of the Canaanites.

CHAPTER XVIII.

WHEN the two great tribes of Judah and Joseph had been located, the one taking the south and the other the middle portion of the country, there seems to have been a pause in the work of distribution. We have no direct statement of the reason, but, from Joshua's words in the third verse of this chapter, we see that the people generally were somewhat to blame. Yet there may have been a good reason for the postponement, such as the breaking out of some formidable insurrection among the enslaved Canaanites (see chap. xvii. 13), or the need of further surveying of the land itself in order to know more exactly the landmarks (see chap. xviii. 4). The people were perhaps to blame only for showing no zeal and readiness to resume and complete the work at the proper time. We are not told how long the interval was between the dividing of the land to the two tribes at Gilgal and the dividing of the land to the seven tribes at Shiloh. We cannot believe that Joshua would have permitted it to be long, however the people in their nomadic habits may have been listless in the matter.

1 AND the whole congregation of the children of
Israel assembled together at Shiloh, and set up the
tabernacle of the congregation there: and the land was
subdued before them.

2 And there remained among the children of Israel
seven tribes, which had not yet received their inheritance.

VER. 1. *Shiloh*, now Seilun, twelve miles soûth of
Shechem and two miles east of the main north and
south road. This retired spot was, nevertheless,
the very centre of the land. Its name ("rest")
is indicative of God's fulfilled promise to his covenant people in settling them in their new land,
and giving them rest from wandering and from
enemies. The place was thus typical of the rest
of the soul in Jesus, who is also designated as
Shiloh in Gen. xlix. 10.

The tabernacle of the congregation. The latter
word is not the same as that in the first part of the
verse. This "ohel moed" may be rendered "tent
of meeting," where the meeting is that of God
and men, rather than of men together.

The land was subdued before them. This con-
firms our first supposition at the beginning of the
notes on this chapter, that there had been some
formidable insurrection of the Canaanites that
broke off the division at Gilgal. When that was
subdued, then the work could go on ; and, moreover,
now there was so complete a tranquillity that the
tabernacle could be safely reared in its place.
Shiloh continued to be the site of the tabernacle
for three centuries, till Samuel's day. In Saul's

3 And Joshua said unto the children of Israel, How long *are* ye slack to go to possess the land which the Lord God of your fathers hath given you?

4 Give out from among you three men for *each* tribe: and I will send them, and they shall rise, and go through the land, and describe it according to the inheritance of them, and they shall come *again* to me.

5 And they shall divide it into seven parts: Judah shall abide in their coast on the south, and the house of Joseph shall abide in their coasts on the north.

6 Ye shall therefore describe the land *into* seven parts, and bring *the description* hither to me, that I may cast lots for you here before the Lord our God.

time the tabernacle was at Nob, and in Solomon's day (before the temple was built) at Gibeon.

Ver. 3. *Slack.* See prefatory note on this chapter.

Ver. 4. A more thorough survey of the land was needed for the exact division called for. *Three men for each tribe*, excluding, of course, Reuben and Gad, but probably including Judah, Ephraim, and Manasseh, as they were interested in the division of the boundaries which actually occurred. The number of surveyors would thus be thirty.

Ver. 5. This seems to be a general statement regarding the two great tribes. They should occupy the relative positions given them, but Judah was to have Simeon and Dan admitted into its inheritance.

Ver. 6. *Describe the land*, probably by enumerating the towns and marking the prominent landmarks. (See ver. 9.) The seven portions having been described, these lots were to be cast, to determine which tribe should receive any given portion.

7 But the Levites have no part among you; for the priesthood of the LORD *is* their inheritance: and Gad, and Reuben, and half the tribe of Manasseh, have received their inheritance beyond Jordan on the east, which Moses the servant of the LORD gave them.

8 ¶ And the men arose, and went away: and Joshua charged them that went to describe the land, saying, Go, and walk through the land, and describe it, and come again to me, that I may here cast lots for you before the LORD in Shiloh.

9 And the men went and passed through the land, and described it by cities into seven parts in a book, and came *again* to Joshua to the host at Shiloh.

10 ¶ And Joshua cast lots for them in Shiloh before the LORD: and there Joshua divided the land unto the children of Israel according to their divisions.

11 ¶ And the lot of the tribe of the children of Benjamin came up according to their families: and the coast of their lot came forth between the children of Judah and the children of Joseph.

12 And their border on the north side was from Jordan; and the border went up to the side of Jericho, on the north side, and went up through the mountains westward; and the goings out thereof were at the wilderness of Beth-aven.

13 And the border went over from thence toward Luz, to the side of Luz (which *is* Beth-el) southward; and the border descended to Ataroth-adar, near the hill that *lieth* on the south side of the nether Beth-horon.

These lots were to be cast as a religious act, with all the solemnity of the high-priest's official presence. (Comp. chap. xiv. 1.)

The Lot of Benjamin.

VER. 11. Benjamin occupied the region left between Judah's northern boundary and Ephraim's southern boundary.

VER. 12, 13. This border is exactly the same with the southern border of Joseph, as given in

14 And the border was drawn *thence*, and compassed the corner of the sea southward, from the hill that *lieth* before Beth-horon southward; and the goings out thereof were at Kirjath-baal (which *is* Kirjath-jearim) a city of the children of Judah. This *was* the west quarter.

15 And the south quarter *was* from the end of Kirjath-jearim, and the border went out on the west, and went out to the well of waters of Nephtoah:

chap. xvi. 1–3 (which see). Read the first part of the thirteenth verse thus: "And the border went over thence (*i.e.*, from Beth-aven) to Luz on the side of Luz (which is Bethel) southward." The two towns called Luz are thus distinguished. (See on chap. xvi. 2.)

VER. 14. A very erroneous idea may be gathered from our version. Benjamin's lot did not reach the sea, but here it is said to "compass the corner of the sea." The Hebrew for "sea" is used for "west," and the right rendering here is, "turned on the west side southward." That is, Benjamin's west boundary left the south boundary of Ephraim near the hill or mountain in front of Beth-horon southwards, and struck south to Kirjath-jearim (for *Kirjath-jearim*, see on chap. ix. 3), a distance of six miles. This west line would run very near to Chephirah.

VER. 15. *From the end of Kirjath-jearim.* Because Kirjath-jearim itself was in Judah.

On the west, i.e., on the west of the south line. So "the border went out on the west" is equivalent to "the border went out or started from the west." It is curious to see how this "yammah" and

8* L

16 And the border came down to the end of the mountain that *lieth* before the valley of the son of Hinnom, *and* which *is* in the valley of the giants on the north, and descended to the valley of Hinnom, to the side of Jebusi on the south, and descended to En-rogel,

17 And was drawn from the north, and went forth to En-shemesh, and went forth toward Geliloth, which *is* over against the going up of Adummim, and descended to the stone of Bohan the son of Reuben,

18 And passed along toward the side over against Arabah northward, and went down unto Arabah:

19 And the border passed along to the side of Beth-hoglah northward: and the out-goings of the border were at the north bay of the salt sea at the south end of Jordan. This *was* the south coast.

20 And Jordan was the border of it on the east side. This *was* the inheritance of the children of Benjamin, by the coasts thereof round about, according to their families.

21 Now the cities of the tribe of the children of Benjamin according to their families, were Jericho, and Beth-hoglah, and the valley of Keziz.

" miyyam," the two opposites (" seawards" and " from the sea "), come to mean virtually the same thing. " Yammah" means literally " seawards " or " westwards," and " miyyam," " from the west," but each is used for " on the west."

VER. 15–19. This south border of Benjamin is the north border of Judah, as given (in the other direction) in chap. xv. 5–9.

VER. 20. The Jordan formed Benjamin's eastern boundary, probably from Wady Nawaimeh to its mouth.

VER. 21. *Jericho.* (See on chap. ii. 2.)

Beth-hoglah. (See on chap. xv. 6.)

The valley of Keziz, or rather " Emek Keziz." This place was probably in the Ghor.

22 And Beth-arabah, and Zemaraim, and Beth-el,
23 And Avim, and Parah, and Ophrah,
24 And Chephar-haammonai, and Ophni, and Gaba;
twelve cities with their villages:
25 Gibeon, and Ramah, and Beeroth,
26 And Mizpeh, and Chephirah, and Mozah,
27 And Rekem, and Irpeel, and Taralah,

VER. 22. *Beth-arabah.* (See on chap. xv. 6.)

Zemaraim, perhaps near Mount Zemaraim of
2 Chron. xiii. 4. If so, then we must look for it
near Bethel. The name is, probably, a relic of
the old Zemarites (Gen. x. 18).

Bethel. (See chap. vii. 2.)

VER. 23. *Avim.* Another form of " Ai."

Parah. Now Farah, on Wady Farah.

Ophrah is probably the same as Ephraim of
2 Chron. xiii. 19, and Ephraim of John xi. 54.
Robinson suggests Taiyibeh as its site, but Taiyibeh
seems to be north of Benjamin's lot.

VER. 24. *Chephar-haammonai* and *Ophni* are not
identified.

Gaba (or Geba) is Jeba, on a height on the
south of Wady es-Suweinit.

VER. 25. *Gibeon.* (See chap. ix. 3.)

Ramah is er-Ram, near Geba.

Beeroth. (See chap. ix. 3.)

VER. 26. *Mizpeh* is now (probably) Neby Samwil, the commanding pinnacle five miles north-west
of Jerusalem.

Chephirah. (See on chap. ix. 3.)

Mozah is not identified.

VER. 27. *Rekem, Irpeel,* and *Taralah* are unknown.

28 And Zelah, Eleph, and Jebusi, (which *is* Jerusalem) Gibeath, *and* Kirjath; fourteen cities with their villages.   This *is* the inheritance of the children of Benjamin according to their families.

VER. 28. *Zelah* and *Eleph* are unknown.

Gibeath, same as " Gibeah of Saul " (1 Sam. xi. 4), or " Gibeah of Benjamin " (Judg. xx. 10), is probably Tuleil el-Ful, a conical hill three miles north of Jerusalem.

Kirjath is perhaps Khirbet el-Kuta, close to Gibeah.

CHAPTER XIX.

1 AND the second lot came forth to Simeon, *even* for the tribe of the children of Simeon according to their families: and their inheritance was within the inheritance of the children of Judah.

The Lot of Simeon.

VER. 1. *To Simeon, for the tribe of the children of Simeon.* This repetition of the tribal name is found with Gad (chap. xiii. 24), with Issachar (ver. 17), and with Naphtali (ver. 32). In the last there is a repetition of the word " children " also.

The full formula, " tribe of the children of —— by their families," is not always given in this enumeration of the distributions. " Tribe " is omitted, of course, with Joseph, because he was really two tribes. Besides this, " tribe " is omitted with Ephraim (chap. xvi. 5), with Benjamin (chap. xviii. 28), with Zebulun (chap. xix. 10, 16), with Issachar (chap. xix. 17), with Naphtali (chap. xix. 32), with Reuben (chap. xiii. 23), with Gad (chap. xiii. 28). Yet with all these, " tribe " is used elsewhere in the enumeration, with the exception of Zebulun only. There can be no reason assigned for these slight differences, and we only notice them here to disprove the idea (held by the Masorites)

2 And they had in their inheritance, Beer-sheba, or Sheba, and Moladah,

3 And Hazar-shual, and Balah, and Azem,

4 And Eltolad, and Bethul, and Hormah,

5 And Ziklag, and Beth-marcaboth, and Hazar-susah,

6 And Beth-lebaoth, and Sharuhen; thirteen cities and their villages:

7 Ain, Remmon, and Ether, and Ashan; four cities and their villages:

8 And all the villages that *were* round about these cities to Baalath-beer, Ramath of the south. This *is* the inheritance of the tribe of the children of Simeon according to their families.

that every word, as such, had its important meaning in the record, and that the omission of any word from a formula was significant.

Within the inheritance of the children of Judah. This was probably not an after-thought, but, when Judah received its limits at the Gilgal allotment, it was doubtless expected that while its borders would not be modified, yet, as occasion might demand, districts within its borders would be given to other tribes.

VER. 2. *Beer-sheba, or Sheba.* Rather, " Beer-sheba and Sheba." Sheba is a different place, called Shema in chap. xv. 26. All these towns have occurred in the list of Judah's towns in chap. xv.

VER. 6. *Thirteen cities.* There are fourteen in the list, but Beer-sheba and Sheba may have been twin cities closely united, and thus counted as one, or there may be here an error in the transcription. (See on chap. xv. 32.)

VER. 8. *These cities, i.e.,* Ain, Remmon, Ether,

9 Out of the portion of the children of Judah *was* the inheritance of the children of Simeon : for the part of the children of Judah was too much for them: therefore the children of Simeon had their inheritance within the inheritance of them.

10 ¶ And the third lot came up for the children of Zebulun according to their families: and the border of their inheritance was unto Sarid:

11 And their border went up toward the sea, and Maralah, and reached to Dabbasheth, and reached to the river that *is* before Jokneam,

and Ashan. These cities with their surroundings were given to Simeon, but the diameter of the circle did not reach to Baalath-beer (or Ramath-negeb, " Ramah of the south "). This Baalath-beer may be either the Bealoth or the Baalah of the list in chap. xv. Van de Velde puts it at Tell-Lekiyeh, north of Beersheba.

VER. 9. *Out of the portion of the children of Judah.* Simeon's eighteen cities lay scattered through the Negeb and Shephelah. They did not form a solid commonwealth. This was in accordance with Jacob's prophecy (Gen. xlix. 7).

The Lot of Zebulun.

VER. 10. *Sarid* is, I take it, the south-west corner of the boundary of Zebulun. It is not identified. I consider ver. 11 as giving the west boundary, ver. 12, the south boundary, ver. 13, the east boundary, and ver. 14, the north boundary. Sarid is probably mentioned so conspicuously as being the nearest point of Zebulun to the tribes already located.

VER. 11. After mentioning Sarid, the west boundary is given from north to south till it

12 And turned from Sarid eastward, toward the sun-
rising, unto the border of Chisloth-tabor, and then
goeth out to Daberath, and goeth up to Japhia,
13 And from thence passeth on along on the east to
Gittah-hepher, to Ittah-kazin, and goeth out to Remmon-methoar to Neah;

reaches Sarid; thus, Maralah, Dabbasheth, and
Wady Jokneam, then comes Sarid, from which in
ver. 12 the south boundary is drawn.

Toward the sea. Rather, "on the west," like
"on the east" in ver. 13.

If the valley of Jiphthah-el is the second wady
north of Wady Abilin (which seems probable),
then I would place *Maralah* at Shefa Omar, on the
ridge above the sea plain, and the phrase, "went
up," would refer to the ascent to Shefa Omar from
the wady north of Abilin.

Dabbasheth may be el-Harbaji on the Wady el-
Malek, near its junction with the Nahr el-Mukutta, and *Wady Jokneam* is the Nahr el-Mukutta
itself.

VER. 12. *Sarid* would thus be somewhere near
Tell el-Thureh.

Chisloth-tabor is undoubtedly Iksal, near Mount
Tabor.

Daberath is Deburieh. The boundary went
north of this place, as Daberath was in Issachar
(chap. xxi. 28).

Japhia we must look for near Khan et-Tujjar.

VER. 13. This verse should read, " And thence
passeth, on the east, eastward of Gath-hepher to
Ittah-kazin." The eastern boundary went up

14 And the border compasseth it on the north side to Hannathon: and the out-goings thereof are in the valley of Jiphthah-el:

15 And Kattath, and Nahallal, and Shimron, and Idalah, and Beth-lehem; twelve cities with their villages.

northward from Japhia, to the eastward of Gath-hepher (or Gittah-hepher), to Ittah-kezin and Rimmon.

Gittah-hepher is el-Meshhad.

Ittah-kazin may be Kefr Kenna.

Remmon-methoar, or Rimmon-hammethoar, is Rummaneh. " Methoar " is not a part of the name, but is a participle meaning " marked off," and the phrase should read, " Rimmon which is marked off (or ' which belongs ') to Neah."

Neah is unknown.

VER. 14. *Compasseth it*, *i.e.*, the inheritance (ver. 10).

Hannathon would probably be Kana el-Jelil.

The valley of Jiphthah-el is the valley going down from Jefat (Jotapata of Josephus) into the Wady Sha'ab.

VER. 15. Keil conjectures from sound reasoning that there is a gap here between ver. 14 and ver. 15, in which seven other cities would be mentioned to make the twelve.

Kattath is unknown.

Nahallal is supposed to be Malul.

Shimron is supposed to be Semmunieh.

Idalah is supposed to be Jeida.

Beth-lehem is now Beit-lahm.

16 This *is* the inheritance of the children of Zebulun according to their families, these cities with their villages.

17 ¶ *And* the fourth lot came out to Issachar, for the children of Issachar according to their families.

18 And their border was toward Jezreel, and Chesulloth, and Shunem,

19 And Hapharaim, and Shihon, and Anaharath,

20 And Rabbith, and Kishion, and Abez,

VER. 16. The territory of Zebulun thus described is a rude square, fifteen miles on each side. The Wady el-Melik and its feeder the Wady el-Bedawi (or Khulladiyeh) divides this territory almost equally into a northern and a southern section. In the southern section is Nazareth, and in the northern is Cana of Galilee. The region is peculiarly sacred (Matt. iv. 15).

The Lot of Issachar.

VER. 18. *Their border was toward Jezreel*, or, "their border was to Jezreel," *i.e.*, included Jezreel.

Jezreel is now Zerin.

Chesulloth is the same, probably, as Chislothtabor of ver. 12.

Shunem is Sulem.

VER. 19. *Hapharaim* is, perhaps, Afuleh.

Shihon is unknown.

Anaharath is, perhaps, en-Na'urah.

VER. 20. *Rabbith* is unknown.

Kishion (or Kishon) was probably on the river Kishon, the el-Mukutta.

Abez is unknown.

21 And Remeth, and En-gannim, and En-haddah, and Beth-pazzez;

22 And the coast reacheth to Tabor, and Shahazimah, and Beth-shemesh; and the out-goings of their border were at Jordan: sixteen cities with their villages.

23 This *is* the inheritance of the tribe of the children of Issachar according to their families, the cities and their villages.

24 ¶ And the fifth lot came out for the tribe of the children of Asher according to their families.

25 And their border was Helkath, and Hali, and Beten, and Achshaph,

VER. 21. *Remeth* is unknown.

En-gannim is, perhaps, Jenin.

En-haddah is, probably, Beit-Kad, west of Gilboa.

VER. 22. *Tabor* (mountain and town) was on the boundary of Zebulun and Issachar.

Shahazimah is unknown.

Beth-shemesh is supposed to be Bessum.

VER. 23. Issachar's portion was the great plain south of a line of latitude running through Tabor, extending to the Jordan behind both Tabor and Gilboa. It was a larger portion than Zebulon's, and remarkable for its fertility.

The Lot of Asher.

VER. 25. Asher's boundary is described from the neighborhood of Achzib (ez-Zib) southward, then the south boundary, then the east, and finally the sea boundary to Achzib, and then some interior towns added. It was a strip of coast sixty miles long, and perhaps in no place extending over eight or ten miles from the sea.

26 And Alammelech, and Amad, and Misheal; and reacheth to Carmel westward, and to Shihor-libnath;

27 And turneth toward the sun-rising to Beth-dagon, and reacheth to Zebulun, and to the valley of Jiphthah-el toward the north side of Beth-emek, and Neiel, and goeth out to Cabul on the left hand,

28 And Hebron, and Rehob, and Hammon, and Kanah, *even* unto great Zidon;

Helkath, Hali, Beten, Achshaph, are supposed to be towns near Akka, but it may be that they are towns in the Dor district south-west of Carmel. If so, the ruins of Hani, east of Tantura, may be Hali, and Iksim may be Achshaph.

VER. 26. *Alammelech* is supposed to be connected with the present Wady Melik.

Amad is supposed to be Haifa.

Misheal is Misalli. Read, "and reacheth to Carmel on the west (or sea) side." That is, Carmel is part of its west frontier.

Shihor-libnath is supposed to be the Belus (Nahr Na'man), which enters the sea by Akka.

VER. 27. *Beth-dagon* must be looked for in the plain of Akka.

Reacheth to Zebulun. Asher's portion probably touched Zebulun's from the neighborhood of Tell el-Kaimon (Jokneam) up to the wady running from Jefat (Jiphthah-el).

Beth-emek and *Neiel* are unknown.

Cabul still bears the same name.

VER. 28. *Hebron* (differently spelled in Hebrew from the Hebron of Judah) is probably the same as Abdon in chap. xxi. 30, and may be sited at Abdeh on the Wady el-Kurn.

29 And *then* the coast turneth to Ramah, and to the strong city Tyre; and the coast turneth to Hosah: and the out-goings thereof are at the sea from the coast to Achzib:

30 Ummah also, and Aphek, and Rehob: twenty and two cities with their villages.

Rehob is unknown.

Hammon is probably Hamul.

Kanah is Kana, eight miles south-east of Tyre.

Unto great Zidon. Perhaps only to its territory, that is, to the river Leontes, which would be Asher's north boundary.

VER. 29. *Ramah* bears the same name, near Tyre.

Tyre. (See on chap. xi. 8.)

Hosah is unknown. Read, "and its outgoings are on the west at the region of Achzib." That is, Achzib forms part of its west frontier.

Achzib is now ez-Zib, just south of the ladder of Tyre.

VER. 30. *Ummah* and *Rehob* are unknown.

Aphek is generally supposed to be Afka, east of Jebeil, but it seems very doubful to me whether the fifty miles of territory from the mouth of the Leontes to Jebeil was ever intended to be divided among the Israelites. (See note on chap. xiii. 4, 5.) I should rather expect to find Ummah, Rehob, and Aphek between Achzib and Akka. The supposed identification of Afka with Asher's Aphek by Robinson and others is the chief argument for extending Asher so very far to the north. But Aphek was a common name. There are cer-

31 This *is* the inheritance of the tribe of the children of Asher according to their families, these cities
with their villages.

32 ¶ The sixth lot came out to the children of Naphtali, *even* for the children of Naphtali according to their
families.

33 And their coast was from Heleph, from Allon to
Zaanannim, and Adami, Nekeb, and Jabneel, unto
Lakum; and the out-goings thereof were at Jordan:

34 And *then* the coast turneth westward to Aznoth-
tabor, and goeth out from thence to Hukkok, and reach-

tainly four others mentioned in the Old Testament
history. We are not, therefore, to lay much stress
on the discovery of an Aphek by the river Adonis,
above the thirty-fourth parallel. That it is the
Aphaca of Eusebius and Sozomen, where the famous temple of Aphrodite stood, there can be no
doubt, but that it is the Aphek of Asher is very
hard to believe.

Twenty and two cities. By leaving out Zidon,
as I have proposed above.

The Lot of Naphtali.

VER. 33. *Heleph* is unknown.

Allon to Zaanannim. Rather, " the oak-forest
at Zaanannim." Zaanannim is near Kedesh (Judg.
iv. 11), north-west of the Huleh.

Adami-nekeb should be read as one word. This
place and *Jabneel* and *Lakum* are unknown. Jabneel may be at Dibbin, and then the Jordan at
Hasbeiya would mark Naphtali's north-eastern
corner.

VER. 34. *Turneth westward*, *i.e.*, from Jordan,
which is Naphtali's east border. This begins the

eth to Zebulun on the south side, and reacheth to Asher
on the west side, and to Judah upon Jordan toward
the sun-rising.

35 And the fenced cities *are* Ziddim, Zer, and Hammath, Rakkath, and Cinneroth,

south boundary, at the Jordan, just south of the
lake of Tiberias.

Aznoth-tabor and *Hukkok* must have been in the
neighborhood of Kefr Sabt. The boundaries of
Zebulun and *Asher* then are touched, extending to
Jotapata (Jefat), and so northward to the Leontes.
So *Zebulun* was Naphtali's south limit, *Asher* its
west limit, and *Judah upon Jordan* its east limit.
Judah upon Jordan is supposed by Von Raumer
to mean the sixty towns of Jair and the lands
appertaining, which he sites upon the east of the
Jordan, opposite Naphtali's lot. Jair was a Judah-
ite, although inheriting in Manasseh. (See 1 Chron.
ii. 5, 21, 22.) Hence his territory, though in
Manasseh, would be called Judah. Keil accepts
this view. It may be that the word " Judah " has
slipped in, and that the text originally stood simply
" to Jordan on the east." (Comp. LXX.)

VER. 35. *Ziddim* is unknown.

Zer I conjecture to be the Chorazin of the
gospels, on the lake. Chorazin is called by Origen
Xώρα Ζιν (Chora-zin), or " the region of Zin."
That Zin should be the same as Zer is very natural.

Hammath is certainly Ammaus, the " Hammam "
below Tiberias.

Rakkath is Kerak, at the south of the lake.

36 And Adamah, and Ramah, and Hazor,
37 And Kedesh, and Edrei, and En-hazor,
38 And Iron, and Migdal-el. Horem, and Beth-anath, and Beth-shemesh; nineteen cities with their villages.
39 This *is* the inheritance of the tribe of the children of Naphtali according to their families, the cities and their villages.
40 ¶ *And* the seventh lot came out for the tribe of the children of Dan according to their families.
41 And the coast of their inheritance was Zorah, and Eshtaol, and Ir-shemesh,
42 And Shaalabbin, and Ajalon, and Jethlah,

Cinneroth was on the little plain south of Mejdel, also on the lake.

VER. 36. *Adamah* was probably in the Ard el-Ahmar.

Ramah is Rameh.

Hazor is Huzzur.

VER. 37. *Kedesh* is Kedes.

Edrei is unknown.

En-hazor is Ain Hazur.

VER. 38. *Iron* is Jarun.

Migdal-el is Magdala (Mejdel) on the lake.

Horem is, perhaps, Hurah.

Beth-anath is, perhaps, Ainata.

Beth-shemeth is Bessum (see on ver. 22), which probably had a district in each tribe, Issachar and Naphtali.

The Lot of Dan.

VER. 41. *Zorah* and *Eshtaol*. (See on chap. xv. 33.)

Ir-shemesh, same as Beth-shemesh (1 Ki. iv. 9. See chap. xv. 10.)

VER. 42. *Shaalabbin* is Selbit, north of Ajalon.

43 And Elon, and Thimnathah, and Ekron,
44 And Eltekeh, and Gibbethon, and Baalath,
45 And Jehud, and Bene-berak, and Gath-rimmon,
46 And Me-jarkon, and Rakkon, with the border before Japho.
47 And the coast of the children of Dan, went out
too little for them: therefore the children of Dan went
up to fight against Leshem, and took it, and smote it
with the edge of the sword, and possessed it, and dwelt
therein, and called Leshem, Dan, after the name of
Dan their father.

Ajalon is Salo.

Jethlah is unknown.

VER. 43. *Elon* is unknown.

Thimnathah (Timnah) and *Ekron*. (See on
chap. xv. 10, 11.)

VER. 44. *Eltekeh* and *Gibbethon* are unknown.

Baalath (Baalah). (See on chap. xv. 11.)

VER. 45. *Jehud* is, perhaps, Jehudiyeh, and *Bene-
berak* is Ibn-Ibrak, both on the north side of Wady
Muzeirah. If so, then *Gath-rimmon* must be
sought in this vicinity. It may be, however, that
Gath-rimmon and Gath are the same, and then we
must look for Jehud and Bene-berak in the vicinity
of Tell es-Safieh.

VER. 46. *Me-jarkon* and *Rakkon* are unknown.

The border before Japho, i.e., Japho (Joppa) and
the border of the sea that lies near it. (Comp.
the phrases like οἱ ἀμφὶ Πρίαμον, so common in the
Greek.)

VER. 47. The Hebrew literally translated is this:
" And the border of the children of Dan went forth
from them, and the children of Dan went up," &c.
The first clause is equivalent to " the children of

9   M

48 This *is* the inheritance of the tribe of the children of Dan according to their families, these cities with their villages.

49 ¶ When they had made an end of dividing the land for inheritance by their coasts, the children of Israel gave an inheritance to Joshua the son of Nun among them:

50 According to the word of the LORD they gave him the city which he asked, *even* Timnath-serah in mount Ephraim: and he built the city, and dwelt therein.

51 These *are* the inheritances which Eleazar the priest, and Joshua the son of Nun, and the heads of the fathers of the tribes of the children of Israel, divided for an inheritance by lot in Shiloh before the LORD, at the door of the tabernacle of the congregation. So they made an end of dividing the country.

Dan went forth from their border." So the LXX understand it. It is a metathesis of subject and object. (Comp. Shakespeare's " His coward lips did from their colour fly.")

The " too little " of our English version is gratuitous, and the " for " is erroneous.

Leshem is Laish. See Judges xviii. for the full account. Laish is Tell el-Kadi, a few miles west of Baneas, at one of the sources of the Jordan, and about one hundred miles distant from Dan's inheritance. This raid upon Leshem was made after Joshua's death, and its story is inserted here to complete the view of Dan's settlement. We see in Judges i. 34, the reason for this movement; to wit, that the Amorites were too strong for Dan, and kept them out of their best territory.

VER. 50. *According to the word of the Lord.* This is not recorded in the Pentateuch, just as the details concerning Caleb's possession are not re-corded there. (See on chap. xiv. 9.)

Timnath-serah (Timnath-heres in Judg. ii. 9) is Tibneh, eight miles north-west of Bethel.

Built, i.e., "built up," or "rebuilt." This chapter ends the account of the distribution of the land.

CHAPTER XX.

IX. The Cities of Refuge.

1 The Lord also spake unto Joshua, saying,

2 Speak to the children of Israel, saying, Appoint out for you cities of refuge, whereof I spake unto you by the hand of Moses:

3 That the slayer that killeth *any* person unawares *and* unwittingly, may flee thither: and they shall be your refuge from the avenger of blood.

4 And when he that doth flee unto one of those cities shall stand at the entering of the gate of the city, and shall declare his cause in the ears of the elders of that city, they shall take him into the city unto them, and give him a place, that he may dwell among them.

5 And if the avenger of blood pursue after him, then they shall not deliver the slayer up into his hand; because he smote his neighbour unwittingly, and hated him not beforetime.

6 And he shall dwell in that city, until he stand before the congregation for judgment, *and* until the death of the high priest that shall be in those days: then shall the slayer return, and come unto his own city, and unto his own house, unto the city from whence he fled.

Ver. 2. *Cities of refuge.* Rather, "*the* cities of refuge," *i.e.*, those referred to in Num. xxxv. 6, 11.

Ver. 3. *Unawares and unwittingly.* Lit., "by mistake in failure of knowledge." That is, where there was no design to commit murder, but the blow was given in ignorance of its result.

Avenger of blood. Heb., "Goël Haddam." For the law of the avenger, see Num. xxxv. It was a

7 ¶ And they appointed Kedesh in Galilee in mount Naphtali, and Shechem in mount Ephraim, and Kirjath-arba, (which *is* Hebron) in the mountain of Judah.

8 And on the other side Jordan by Jericho eastward, they assigned Bezer in the wilderness upon the plain

system which checked revenge, by giving the avenger a sacred character, and, by the cities of refuge, protected the innocent from harm.

They shall be. So "shall stand," "shall declare," "shall take," &c., in the next verse. These are all preterites in the Hebrew, as marking a system already established, but now only made available.

VER. 7. *And they appointed Kedesh.* This in Hebrew is a paronomasia, "wayya*kedishu* eth-*Kedesh.*" For Kedesh, see chap. xix. 37.

Galilee. Heb., "Galil" (circle). In Isaiah "Gelil ha-goyim" (Galilee of the Gentiles), because so many foreigners dwelt in that northern part of Palestine.

Mount Naphtali, i.e., the mountainous portion of Naphtali, as distinguished from that part of Naphtali lying in the Jordan valley.

Shechem. The well-known central town of Palestine, between Ebal and Gerizim, mentioned frequently in the patriarchal history, the Sychar of our Lord's day, now Nablus (Neapolis).

Mount Ephraim. The mountain district of Ephraim: Manasseh and Benjamin was so called. Shechem was in Ephraim (Josh. xxi. 20, 21).

Hebron. (See on chap. x. 3.)

VER. 8. These cities of refuge on the east side of Jordan had already been appointed by

out of the tribe of Reuben, and Ramoth in Gilead out
of the tribe of Gad, and Golan in Bashan out of the
tribe of Manasseh.

9 These were the cities appointed for all the children of Israel, and for the stranger that sojourneth

Moses (Deut. iv. 43). *Bezer* is not yet identified,
though we may hope that the American Exploring
Expedition now engaged in triangulating the territory east of Jordan may find this interesting site.
Bezer is called Bezer in the wilderness (Midbar),
in the plain (Mishor) of Reuben. The *Mishor*
would appear to be the plain between Heshbon
and the Wady Zerka Main (now el-Belka), and
the *Midbar* of this Mishor would be its eastern
frontier. If so, we must look for Bezer near Jebel
Jalul.

Ramoth in Gilead. It is usual to consider es-
Salt, three miles south of Jebel Osha, to be Ramoth-
Gilead, but this site is not near enough to Damascus and Argob to suit the various statements in
the Old Testament concerning it. If Ramoth-Gilead and Ramath-Mizpeh (Josh. xiii. 21) are the
same, and if Jacob's Mizpeh is to be identified with
this, then we have an additional argument for believing that Ramoth-Gilead is to be placed at or
near Gerash, according to Ewald and the Jewish
traveller Parchi.*

Golan is not identified, but it gave name to the
well-known province of Gaulonitis (Jaulan), east
of the lake of Galilee.

* Since the above was written, Mr. Paine, of the American
Expedition, informs me that he has identified Ramoth-Gilead near
Gerash.

among them, that whosoever killeth *any* person at unawares might flee thither, and not die by the hand of
the avenger of blood, until he stood before the congregation.

VER. 9. The fugitive, on arriving at the city of
refuge, reported himself, and was protected until
the assembly of his own town could pass judgment
in the case. Thus much is alluded to in this verse.
In ver. 6 reference is made to the death of the
high-priest. This has regard to the case of the
slayer if *innocent*. If he were *guilty* of intentional
murder, the city of refuge extended no protection
over him after the assembly of his own town had
convicted him. But if *innocent*, then he was taken
back to the city of refuge, and abode there, protected, till the then high-priest died.

CHAPTER XXI.

X. The Levitical Cities.

1 Then came near the heads of the fathers of the Levites unto Eleazar the priest, and unto Joshua the son of Nun, and unto the heads of the fathers of the tribes of the children of Israel;

2 And they spake unto them at Shiloh in the land of Canaan, saying, The Lord commanded by the hand of Moses to give us cities to dwell in, with the suburbs thereof for our cattle.

3 And the children of Israel gave unto the Levites out of their inheritance, at the commandment of the Lord, these cities and their suburbs.

4 And the lot came out for the families of the Kohathites: and the children of Aaron the priest, *which were* of the Levites, had by lot out of the tribe of Judah, and out of the tribe of Simeon, and out of the tribe of Benjamin, thirteen cities.

Ver. 1. *Heads of the fathers.* (See on chap. xiv. 1.)

Ver. 2. *At Shiloh.* The occasion is the same as that mentioned in chap. xviii. 1. We need not imagine any new gathering at Shiloh. But this was part of the process of distribution and assignment.

In the land of Canaan. They were actually in the land promised. (See Num. xxxiv. 29.)

The Lord commanded by the hand of Moses. (See Num. xxxv. 2.)

Ver. 4. The children of Levi were Kohath,

5 And the rest of the children of Kohath *had* by lot out of the families of the tribe of Ephraim, and out of the tribe of Dan, and out of the half-tribe of Manasseh, ten cities.

6 And the children of Gershon *had* by lot out of the families of the tribe of Issachar, and out of the tribe of Asher, and out of the tribe of Naphtali, and out of the half-tribe of Manasseh in Bashan, thirteen cities.

7 The children of Merari by their families *had* out of the tribe of Reuben, and out of the tribe of Gad, and out of the tribe of Zebulun, twelve cities.

8 And the children of Israel gave by lot unto the Levites these cities with their suburbs, as the LORD commanded by the hand of Moses.

9 ¶ And they gave out of the tribe of the children of Judah, and out of the tribe of the children of Simeon, these cities which are *here* mentioned by name,

10 Which the children of Aaron, *being* of the families of the Kohathites, *who were* of the children of Levi, had: for theirs was the first lot.

11 And they gave them the city of Arba the father

Gershon, and Merari (Gen. xlvi. 11). Out of the Kohathites. came the priestly family of Aaron. This priestly portion of Kohath received its thirteen cities in Judah, Simeon, and Benjamin.

VER. 5. The rest of Kohath's family received ten cities further north, in Ephraim and Manasseh, and also in Dan on the west.

VER. 6. Gershon received thirteen cities still further north, in Issachar, Asher, Naphtali, and across Jordan in Manasseh.

VER. 7. Merari received twelve cities in the southern part of the trans-Jordanic territory (opposite Ephraim, Manasseh, and Judah), in Reuben and Gad, and also in Zebulun on the west side (in the midst of the Gershonite cities).

VER. 11. *And they gave them*, &c. As the forty-
9*

of Anak (which *city is* Hebron) in the hill-*country* of Judah, with the suburbs thereof round about it.

12 But the fields of the city, and the villages thereof, gave they to Caleb the son of Jephunneh for his possession.

13 ¶ Thus they gave to the children of Aaron the priest, Hebron with her suburbs, *to be* a city of refuge for the slayer; and Libnah with her suburbs,

14 And Jattir with her suburbs, and Eshtemoa with her suburbs,

15 And Holon with her suburbs, and Debir with her suburbs,

16 And Ain with her suburbs, and Juttah with her suburbs, *and* Beth-shemesh with her suburbs; nine cities out of those two tribes.

17 And out of the tribe of Benjamin, Gibeon with her suburbs, Geba with her suburbs,

18 Anathoth with her suburbs, and Almon with her suburbs; four cities.

19 All the cities of the children of Aaron, the priests, *were* thirteen cities with their suburbs.

20 ¶ And the families of the children of Kohath, the Levites which remained of the children of Kohath, even they had the cities of their lot out of the tribe of Ephraim.

21 For they gave them Shechem with her suburbs in mount Ephraim, *to be* a city of refuge for the slayer; and Gezer with her suburbs,

22 And Kibzaim with her suburbs, and Beth-horon with her suburbs ; four cities.

23 And out of the tribe of Dan, Eltekeh with her suburbs, Gibbethon with her suburbs,

24 Aijalon with her suburbs, Gath-rimmon with her suburbs; four cities.

eight cities here enumerated have been mostly described before, when their names occurred in the settlement of the tribes, notes will only be given on any new name or circumstance mentioned.

VER. 18. *Anathoth* is Anata.

Almon is unknown.

VER. 22. *Kibzaim* is unknown.

25 And out of the half-tribe of Manasseh, Tanach with her suburbs, and Gath-rimmon with her suburbs; two cities.

26 All the cities *were* ten with their suburbs, for the families of the children of Kohath that remained.

27 ¶ And unto the children of Gershon, of the families of the Levites, out of the *other* half-tribe of Manasseh *they gave* Golan in Bashan with her suburbs, *to be a* city of refuge for the slayer, and Beesh-terah with her suburbs; two cities.

28 And out of the tribe of Issachar, Kishon with her suburbs, Dabareh with her suburbs,

29 Jarmuth with her suburbs, Engannim with her suburbs; four cities.

30 And out of the tribe of Asher, Mishal with her suburbs, Abdon with her suburbs,

31 Helkath with her suburbs, and Rehob with her suburbs; four cities.

32 And out of the tribe of Naphtali, Kedesh in Galilee with her suburbs, *to be* a city of refuge for the slayer; and Hammoth-dor with her suburbs, and Kartan with her suburbs; three cities.

VER. 25. *Gath-rimmon.* Gath-rimmon was in Dan, and is already given in the previous verse. This mention of it is undoubtedly a copyist's error. The name should be (as in 1 Chron. vi. 70) Bileam (the Ibleam of chap. xvii. 11).

VER. 27. *Beesh-terah* is "Ashtaroth" in 1 Chron. vi. 71. It was probably Ashteroth Karnaim. (See on chap. xiii. 12, and comp. Gen. xiv. 5.)

VER. 32. *Hammoth-dor* is Hammath in chap. xix. 35.

Kartan may be Migdal-el of chap. xix. 38, and, as the Levitical portion, may have been (in Migdal-minnith) the later Dalmanutha (Mark viii. 10). Migdal-minnith would mean "the tower of the allotment," and Migdal-el, "the tower of God."

33 All the cities of the Gershonites, according to their families, *were* thirteen cities with their suburbs.

34 ¶ And unto the families of the children of Merari, the rest of the Levites, out of the tribe of Zebulun, Jokneam with her suburbs, and Kartah with her suburbs,

35 Dimnah with her suburbs, Nahalal with her suburbs; four cities.

36 And out of the tribe of Reuben, Bezer with her suburbs, and Jahazah with her suburbs,

37 Kedemoth with her suburbs, and Mephaath with her suburbs; four cities.

38 And out of the tribe of Gad, Ramoth in Gilead with her suburbs, *to be* a city of refuge for the slayer; and Mahanaim with her suburbs,

39 Heshbon with her suburbs, Jazer with her suburbs; four cities in all.

40 So all the cities for the children of Merari by their families, which were remaining of the families of the Levites, were *by* their lot twelve cities.

41 All the cities of the Levites within the possession of the children of Israel *were* forty and eight cities with their suburbs.

42 These cities were every one with their suburbs round about them. Thus *were* all these cities.

43 ¶ And the LORD gave unto Israel all the land which he sware to give unto their fathers: and they possessed it, and dwelt therein.

44 And the LORD gave them rest round about, according to all that he sware unto their fathers: and there stood not a man of all their enemies before them; the LORD delivered all their enemies into their hand.

45 There failed not aught of any good thing which the LORD had spoken unto the house of Israel; all came to pass.

Kartan is not given in the list of Naphtali's towns in chap. xix. If this conjecture be true, then Dalmanutha and Magdala on the west shore of the lake of Galilee would be the same, and Kartan would be its original name.

VER. 34. *Kartah* is unknown.

VER. 35. *Dimnah* is unknown.

CHAPTER XXII.

XI. THE RETURN OF THE TWO TRIBES AND A HALF.

1 THEN Joshua called the Reubenites, and the Gadites, and the half-tribe of Manasseh,

AT the close of the preceding chapter we were
told of the complete possession of the promised
land by Israel, and the perfect peace which the
tribes enjoyed. It is true, many Canaanites remained in various parts of the country, some of
them in strongholds; but their number was com-
paratively small, and their presence was due to
Israel's neglect and not to the Lord's withdrawal
of his hand. Every good thing which the Lord
had spoken unto the house of Israel had been given,
but they had failed to make a thorough work with
the divine supply of strength. When at Shiloh the
distribution of the land had been perfected, the
Reubenites, Gadites, and Manassites of the trans-
Jordanic region, who had faithfully for seven years
continued with their brethren in the subjugation
of the western country, are dismissed by Joshua to
their homes. As this return gave rise to a remarkable incident, which evinced the faithfulness
of Israel, its details are carefully recorded in this
chapter.

2 And said unto them, Ye have kept all that Moses the servant of the LORD commanded you, and have obeyed my voice in all that I commanded you:

3 Ye have not left your brethren these many days unto this day, but have kept the charge of the commandment of the LORD your God.

4 And now the LORD your God hath given rest unto your brethren, as he promised them: therefore now return ye, and get you unto your tents, *and* unto the land of your possession, which Moses the servant of the LORD gave you on the other side Jordan.

5 But take diligent heed to do the commandment and the law, which Moses the servant of the LORD charged you, to love the LORD your God, and to walk in all his ways, and to keep his commandments, and to cleave unto him, and to serve him with all your heart, and with all your soul.

6 So Joshua blessed them, and sent them away; and they went unto their tents.

7 Now to the *one* half of the tribe of Manasseh, Moses had given *possession* in Bashan: but unto the

VER. 2. They had equally obeyed the Lord through the mouth of Moses and of Joshua.

VER. 4. *Tents.* It is probable that some time elapsed before their cities on the east side were rebuilt; and, indeed, it is likely that the two tribes and a half used permanently to some extent the nomadic tent-life, as they were especially concerned with the care of cattle.

VER. 5. *The commandment and the law.* The former refers to all the special orders communicated through Moses and Joshua, and the latter to the written law.

To love, &c. The great purpose of commandment and law is here given, showing that God asked of them no formalism, but the preparation of the heart before him.

other half thereof gave Joshua among their brethren on this side Jordan westward. And when Joshua sent them away also unto their tents, then he blessed them,

8 And he spake unto them, saying, Return with much riches unto your tents, and with very much cattle, with silver, and with gold, and with brass, and with iron, and with very much raiment: divide the spoil of your enemies with your brethren.

9 ¶ And the children of Reuben, and the children of Gad, and the half-tribe of Manasseh returned, and departed from the children of Israel out of Shiloh, which *is* in the land of Canaan, to go unto the country of Gilead, to the land of their possession, whereof they were possessed, according to the word of the LORD by the hand of Moses.

10 ¶ And when they came unto the borders of Jordan, that *are* in the land of Canaan, the children of Reuben, and the children of Gad, and the half-tribe of Manasseh built there an altar by Jordan, a great altar to see to.

11 ¶ And the children of Israel heard say, Behold, the children of Reuben, and the children of Gad, and the half-tribe of Manasseh, have built an altar over against the land of Canaan, in the borders of Jordan, at the passage of the children of Israel.

12 And when the children of Israel heard *of it*, the whole congregation of the children of Israel gathered themselves together at Shiloh, to go up to war against them.

VER. 8. *With your brethren,* i.e., those who had remained at home to guard the eastern side. (See on chap. i. 14.)

VER. 9. *Land of Canaan,* i.e., the west side of the Jordan.

Country of Gilead, i.e., the east side of Jordan.

VER. 11. *Over against the land of Canaan.* Rather, " in front of the land of Canaan," i.e., on its extreme edge. The altar, we see from ver 10, was on the west bank, in the land of Canaan. (See also on ver. 9.)

VER. 12. The whole people on the west side are

13 And the children of Israel sent unto the children of Reuben, and to the children of Gad, and to the half-tribe of Manasseh into the land of Gilead, Phinehas the son of Eleazar the priest,

14 And with him ten princes, of each chief house a prince throughout all the tribes of Israel; and each one *was* an head of the house of their fathers among the thousands of Israel.

15 ¶ And they came unto the children of Reuben, and to the children of Gad, and to the half-tribe of Manasseh, unto the land of Gilead, and they spake with them, saying,

aroused most rightfully, for the act of the two and a half tribes seemed to be a direct rebellion against God's authority, for he had established *one only altar* for the whole of Israel. Although they afterwards explained their act as done with no purpose of making the altar a sacrificial altar (ver. 23), yet they certainly did a most imprudent and rash thing in building an altar at all. They should have asked of the Lord through the high-priest, before forming so dangerous a precedent. (See a like error of Gideon's regarding the ephod at Ophrah, Judg. viii. 27.) The readiness of Israel to war upon their offending brethren was a readiness to preserve the integrity of Jehovah's worship.

VER. 13, 14. The delegation, composed of the high-priest's son and ten tribal heads, showed Israel's estimate of the importance of the occasion, and also their wise use of peaceable means before war.

VER. 15. *Unto the land of Gilead.* The delegation find the two tribes and a half already across Jordan, and in their territories. The conference was probably had with a representative

16 Thus saith the whole congregation of the LORD, What trespass *is* this that ye have committed against the God of Israel, to turn away this day from following the LORD, in that ye have builded you an altar, that ye might rebel this day against the LORD?

17 *Is* the iniquity of Peor too little for us, from which we are not cleansed until this day, although there was a plague in the congregation of the LORD,

18 But that ye must turn away this day from following the LORD? and it will be, *seeing* ye rebel to-day against the LORD, that to-morrow he will be wroth with the whole congregation of Israel.

19 Notwithstanding, if the land of your possession *be* unclean, *then* pass ye over unto the land of the possession of the LORD, wherein the LORD'S tabernacle

assembly of the two tribes and a half at some central spot, like Ramoth-Gilead.

VER. 16. They accuse the two tribes and a half of rebellion, and give the altar as proof.

VER. 17. *The iniquity of Peor, i.e.,* the iniquity in joining the worshippers of Baal-peor (Num. xxv. 3).

From which we are not cleansed. They must allude to moral traces of that fearful lapse still cropping out among the people, after seven years.

Plague. The plague which slew twenty-four thousand Israelites because of that sin. (See Num. xxv.) Some were spared, it seems, who still maintained a tainted life.

VER. 18. " If one member suffer, all the members suffer with it " (1 Cor. xii. 26). This was the rule in the old church, as in the new.

VER. 19. This verse contains a clear allusion to the selfish act of the two tribes and a half in securing the east side of Jordan. It was not *in the land*

N

dwelleth, and take possession among us: but rebel not against the LORD, nor rebel against us, in building you an altar beside the altar of the LORD our God.

20 Did not Achan the son of Zerah commit a trespass in the accursed thing, and wrath fell on all the congregation of Israel? and that man perished not alone in his iniquity.

21 ¶ Then the children of Reuben, and the children of Gad, and the half-tribe of Manasseh answered, and said unto the heads of the thousands of Israel,

22 The LORD God of gods, the LORD God of gods, he knoweth, and Israel he shall know; if *it be* in rebellion, or if in transgression against the LORD, (save us not this day,)

of the possession of Jehovah, and hence there is still an opportunity for the two tribes and a half to give up the trans-Jordanic country and settle in the land originally designed for them, the promised land, the land of Canaan. (See on chap. i. 2, and i. 13.) This altar-building was a new instance of the evils resulting from a wrong course at the start.

VER. 20. Achan's sin and its effect upon many is a second illustration of the fearful danger of sinning against God's commands to Israel. The thirty-six who perished before Ai lost their lives through Achan's sin.

VER. 21. *Heads of the thousands of Israel, i.e.,* "heads of the house of their fathers among the thousands of Israel," as in ver. 14. An abbreviated form.

VER. 22. *The Lord God of gods.* Rather, "God, the great God, Jehovah." This repetition of " El, Elohim, Jehovah," shows the great earnestness of the denial.

Save us not this day. A direct cry to God, in-

23 That we have built us an altar to turn from following the LORD, or if to offer thereon burnt-offering, or meat-offering, or if to offer peace-offerings thereon, let the LORD himself require *it;*

24 And if we have not *rather* done it for fear of *this* thing, saying, In time to come your children might speak unto our children, saying, What have ye to do with the LORD God of Israel?

25 For the LORD hath made Jordan a border between us and you, ye children of Reuben and children of Gad; ye have no part in the LORD. So shall your children make our children cease from fearing the LORD.

26 Therefore we said, Let us now prepare to build us an altar, not for burnt-offering, nor for sacrifice:

27 But *that* it *may be* a witness between us, and you, and our generations after us, that we might do the service of the LORD before him with our burnt-offerings, and with our sacrifices, and with our peace-offerings; that your children may not say to our children in time to come, Ye have no part in the LORD.

28 Therefore said we, that it shall be, when they should *so* say to us or to our generations in time to come, that we may say *again*, Behold the pattern of the altar of the LORD, which our fathers made, not for burnt-offerings, nor for sacrifices; but it *is* a witness between us and you.

29 God forbid that we should rebel against the LORD, and turn this day from following the LORD, to build an altar for burnt-offerings, for meat-offerings, or for sacrifices, beside the altar of the LORD our God that *is* before his tabernacle.

terjected in the midst of their speech to Joshua, showing their emotion. They exclaim to God, "Be no longer our Saviour, if we are guilty of rebellion in this."

VER. 24. *For fear of this thing.* Rather, "from anxiety [same word as that translated 'heaviness' in Prov. xii. 25], from a cause."

VER. 27. *That we might do the service of the Lord before him*, i.e., at Shiloh.

VER. 28. *Pattern.* Rather, "copy."

30 ¶ And when Phinehas the priest, and the princes of the congregation, and heads of the thousands of Israel which *were* with him, heard the words that the children of Reuben, and the children of Gad, and the children of Manasseh spake, it pleased them.

31 And Phinehas the son of Eleazar the priest said unto the children of Reuben, and to the children of Gad, and to the children of Manasseh, This day we perceive that the LORD *is* among us, because ye have not committed this trespass against the LORD: now ye have delivered the children of Israel out of the hand of the LORD.

32 ¶ And Phinehas the son of Eleazar the priest, and the princes, returned from the children of Reuben, and from the children of Gad, out of the land of Gilead, unto the land of Canaan, to the children of Israel, and brought them word again.

33 And the thing pleased the children of Israel; and the children of Israel blessed God, and did not intend to go up against them in battle, to destroy the land wherein the children of Reuben and Gad dwelt.

34 And the children of Reuben and the children of Gad called the altar *Ed:* for it *shall be* a witness between us that the LORD *is* God.

VER. 30. *It pleased them.* Lit., "it was good in their eyes." It did not please them that they had built the altar, but that they had not intended any rebellion or transgression.

VER. 31. Phinehas argues from this happy escape from expected evil, and from the proof that the two tribes and a half were loyal to God, to the presence of God among them, a connection of argument most true and most worthy of note.

VER. 34. *Ed.* This word, which means "witness," occurs only once in the Hebrew. The verse should read, "called the altar, 'This is a witness between us that Jehovah is God.'" This whole long name was given to the altar. In Hebrew it is "Edhu benothenu ki yehowah ha-elohim."

CHAPTER XXIII.

XII. JOSHUA'S TWO FAREWELL ADDRESSES. (Chap. xxiii. to xxiv.)

1 AND it came to pass, a long time after that the LORD had given rest unto Israel from all their enemies round about, that Joshua waxed old *and* stricken in age.

VER. 1. *A long time after* — *Joshua waxed old and stricken in age.* The latter expression is used at chap. xiii. 1, in reference to the time prior to the distribution of the land, and when Joshua was probably eighty-seven years old. (See note on l. c.) The former expression, however, leads us forward to some period near Joshua's death, perhaps twenty years after the distribution, and when Joshua was one hundred and seven years old. He may have been anticipating his departure as very near, and felt constrained to use his great influence to warn the nation, before he should leave them for ever. He finds no fault, which fact shows that the early days of the Hebrew commonwealth were pure and faithful days, but he saw that the large number of Canaanites still resident in the land would be (unless special care were taken) a source of sin and ruin to the chosen people. Against this danger he desires to guard them. Probably no man ever

2 And Joshua called for all Israel, *and* for their elders, and for their heads, and for their judges, and for their officers, and said unto them, I am old *and* stricken in age:

3 And ye have seen all that the LORD your God hath done unto all these nations because of you; for the LORD your God *is* he that hath fought for you.

spoke with more moral power to a nation than did Joshua. His influence must have been greater even than that of Moses, as he had completed the work of settling the people as a compact commonwealth, and they felt every day the beneficent results of his grand leadership. With deep reverence and affection they must have hung upon his words, — words that must have had much to do with the comparative purity of the nation for the first centuries of its existence. Joshua's honest, unselfish, godly, and heroic character added to the lustre of his deeds and his influence over all Israel.

VER. 2. *All Israel*, that is, their *elders, heads, judges, officers*, as representatives of the entire nation. (See chap. i. 10, and viii. 33.) This seems to be the order of gradation (ascending series) in the executive powers of the tribes, elders, however, being the generic name for all. This solemn assembly was probably held at Shiloh, as the governmental centre of the nation. Perhaps Joshua took advantage of a national assembly of representatives, and called its members together to hear his farewell words to the people.

VER. 3. *Because of you.* Lit., " From before you." Note here and in ver. 10 the emphasis

4 Behold, I have divided unto you by lot these nations that remain, to be an inheritance for your tribes, from Jordan, with all the nations that I have cut off, even unto the great sea westward.

5 And the LORD your God, he shall expel them from before you, and drive them from out of your sight; and ye shall possess their land, as the LORD your God hath promised unto you.

6 Be ye therefore very courageous to keep and to do all that is written in the book of the law of Moses, that ye turn not aside therefrom *to* the right hand or *to* the left;

7 That ye come not among these nations, these that remain among you; neither make mention of the name of their gods, nor cause to swear *by them*, neither serve them, nor bow yourselves unto them:

8 But cleave unto the LORD your God, as ye have done unto this day.

which Joshua lays upon God's fighting for them. The whole matter of destroying the Canaanites was God's, not theirs.

VER. 4. *With all the nations that I have cut off.* Rather, " even all the nations that I have cut off." These nations that remained had been cut off; that is, they had ceased to have any proper nationality, and were represented only by scattered communities.

VER. 5. *Drive them from out of your sight.* Rather, " dispossess them from before you."

VER. 6, 7. Compare chap. i. 7, for the order of thought.

Serving the gods is sacrificing to them; *bowing* is praying.

VER. 8. *As ye have done unto this day.* A noble testimony for the nation.

9 For the LORD hath driven out from before you great nations and strong: but *as for* you, no man hath been able to stand before you unto this day.

10 One man of you shall chase a thousand: for the LORD your God, he *it is* that fighteth for you, as he hath promised you.

11 Take good heed therefore unto yourselves, that ye love the LORD your God.

12 Else if ye do in any wise go back, and cleave unto the remnant of these nations, *even* these that remain among you, and shall make marriages with them, and go in unto them, and they to you:

13 Know for a certainty that the LORD your God will no more drive out *any of* these nations from before you: but they shall be snares and traps unto you, and scourges in your sides, and thorns in your eyes, until ye perish from off this good land which the LORD your God hath given you.

14 And behold, this day I *am* going the way of all the earth; and ye know in all your hearts and in all your souls, that not one thing hath failed of all the good things which the LORD your God spake concerning you; all are come to pass unto you, *and* not one thing hath failed thereof.

VER. 9. *But as for you.* Rather, " *and* as for you."

VER. 11. *That ye love the Lord your God.* It is remarkable that with such repeated appeals to set the *affections* on God, the Jewish system is asserted to be a mere formal ritualism.

VER. 14. This begins a repetition of a part of what he has already said, but in it he emphasizes the dangers of abandoning Jehovah.

All the earth, *i.e.*, all the inhabitants of the earth.

Hearts — souls (literally, *hearts — breaths*), an idiom for thoroughness of conviction.

15 Therefore it shall come to pass, *that* as all good things are come upon you, which the LORD your God promised you; so shall the LORD bring upon you all evil things, until he have destroyed you from off this good land which the LORD your God hath given you.

16 When ye have transgressed the covenant of the LORD your God, which he commanded you, and have gone and served other gods, and bowed yourselves to them; then shall the anger of the LORD be kindled against you, and ye shall perish quickly from off the good land which he hath given unto you.

VER. 15. *So shall the Lord bring upon you all evil things*, *i.e.*, in case of your failure to cleave to him (as is expressed in the next verse).

VER. 16. The repetition of *good land* in verses 13, 15, and 16 reminds us of the fact that Palestine, when under the favoring care of God, must have been one of the most fertile lands on earth. Its varied climate (as between the mountains and low plains) gave it variety of production, its hills admitting a thorough system of terracing, enabled a very complete occupation of the land for agricultural purposes, and choice exposures could be found for such vegetation as needed more or less influence of the sun, while fountains broke forth on every side and supplied abundantly the land with moisture.

10

CHAPTER XXIV.

1 AND Joshua gathered all the tribes of Israel to Shechem, and called for the elders of Israel, and for their heads and for their judges, and for their officers; and they presented themselves before God.

THIS chapter brings before us another representative assembly, at Shechem this time, and not at Shiloh, in which Joshua renews the covenant between the people and God, as he had done nearly thirty years before in the same place. (See chap. viii. 30–35.) The former address of Joshua seems to have been delivered in the belief that he was soon to leave· this world, and was prompted by his ardent desire for the purity of the people, who would (he knew) be sorely tempted away from God by the idolatrous population among them. *This* address, however, and the assembly at which it was delivered, were appointed by divine direction, as we see by the phrase, " before God," in ver. 1, and the formula, " thus saith Jehovah, God of Israel," in ver. 2. The former occasion was (so to speak) a private conference of Joshua with Israel. *This* occasion was an official conference, in which Joshua acted as the divine legate.

VER. 1. *Shechem*, the place made a sanctuary by Abraham on entering the land·(Gen. xii. 6, 7), and again by Jacob (Gen. xxxiii. 20), and still

2 And Joshua said unto all the people, Thus saith the LORD God of Israel, Your fathers dwelt on the other side of the flood in old time, *even* Terah, the father of Abraham, and the father of Nachor: and they served other gods.

3 And I took your father Abraham from the other side of the flood, and led him throughout all the land of Canaan, and multiplied his seed, and gave him Isaac.

4 And I gave unto Isaac, Jacob and Esau: and I gave unto Esau mount Seir, to possess it; but Jacob and his children went down into Egypt.

5 I sent Moses also and Aaron, and I plagued Egypt, according to that which I did among them: and afterward I brought you out.

6 And I brought your fathers out of Egypt: and ye came unto the sea; and the Egyptians pursued after your fathers with chariots and horsemen unto the Red sea.

7 And when they cried unto the LORD, he put darkness between you and the Egyptians, and brought

again made the scene of the renewal of the covenant when the nation Israel entered upon possession of the land (chap. viii. 30–35). As the very centre of the land, also, it was a fitting spot for the solemn ceremony to be enacted.

Elders — heads — judges — officers. (See on chap. xxiii. 2.)

Before God. Not before the tabernacle which was at Shiloh. That would have been "before Jehovah." But at the command of God, to worship him and take part in a religious act.

VER. 2. *The flood.* Lit., "the river," *i.e.,* the Euphrates.

VER. 3. *Throughout all the land of Canaan,* in order to survey the land promised to his posterity (See Gen. xii.)

the sea upon them, and covered them; and your eyes have seen what I have done in Egypt: and ye dwelt in the wilderness a long season.

8 And I brought you into the land of the Amorites, which dwelt on the other side Jordan; and they fought with you: and I gave them into your hand, that ye might possess their land; and I destroyed them from before you.

9 Then Balak the son of Zippor, king of Moab, arose and warred against Israel, and sent and called Balaam the son of Beor to curse you:

10 But I would not hearken unto Balaam; therefore he blessed you still: so I delivered you out of his hand.

11 And ye went over Jordan, and came unto Jericho: and the men of Jericho fought against you, the Amorites, and the Perizzites, and the Canaanites, and the Hittites, and the Girgashites, the Hivites, and the Jebusites, and I delivered them into your hand.

12 And I sent the hornet before you, which drave them out from before you, *even* the two kings of the Amorites: *but* not with thy sword, nor with thy bow.

VER. 11. *The Amorites*, &c. There seems to be an apposition here with " the men (or possessors) of Jericho." Jericho, as an important frontier city, may have had in it representatives of all the seven nations of Canaan for defence against Israel. Notice that the Girgashites appear here at Jericho, who afterward disappear. (See note on chap. ix. 1.)

VER. 12. This verse seems to be out of place. It should be between the eighth and ninth verses, as it refers to the action against Sihon and Og. The *homoeoteleuton* will account for the error in transcription.

Hornet. (See Ex. xxiii. 28, and Deut. vii. 20.) A figurative expression for the tribulation God

13 And I have given you a land for which ye did not labour, and cities which ye built not, and ye dwell in them; of the vineyards and olive-yards which ye planted not do ye eat.

14 ¶ Now therefore fear the LORD, and serve him in sincerity and in truth: and put away the gods which your fathers served on the other side of the flood, and in Egypt; and serve ye the LORD.

caused among the people of Canaan in preparation for Israel's entrance into the land. Some of this tribulation consisted of their fear of the advancing Israelites (see chap. ii. 9–11), and perhaps some consisted of inter-tribal wars and local pestilences.

VER. 14. The marvellous history so clearly and succinctly recounted was the natural preface for the exhortation which here begins.

Flood. (See on ver. 2.)

Put away the gods. This seems to imply that Israel was beginning to think less evil of the idolatry around them. Perhaps some of the idols of the subdued Canaanites had been preserved as spoil, or had been received as curiosities or ornaments, and God would nip the mischief in the bud. They should put away these objects altogether, for they would tempt them to regard idolatry as a small evil, and so prepare the way for their own idolatrous habits. As, however, the gods they were to put away were the gods which their fathers served on the other side of the Euphrates and in Egypt, it is more probable that they had kept some of the old teraphim (see Gen. xxxi. 34) of Syria and idolatrous trinkets of Egypt as heirlooms among their families. (Comp. Amos v. 26.)

15 And if it seem evil unto you to serve the LORD, choose you this day whom ye will serve, whether the gods which your fathers served that *were* on the other side of the flood, or the gods of the Amorites in whose land ye dwell: but as for me and my house, we will serve the LORD.

16 And the people answered, and said, God forbid that we should forsake the LORD, to serve other gods;

17 For the LORD our God, he *it is* that brought us up, and our fathers, out of the land of Egypt, from the house of bondage, and which did those great signs in our sight, and preserved us in all the way wherein we went, and among all the people through whom we passed:

18 And the LORD drave out from before us all the people, even the Amorites which dwelt in the land: *therefore* will we also serve the LORD; for he *is* our God.

19 And Joshua said unto the people, Ye cannot serve the LORD: for he *is* an holy God: he *is* a jealous God; he will not forgive your transgressions, nor your sins.

20 If ye forsake the LORD, and serve strange gods, then he will turn and do you hurt, and consume you, after that he hath done you good.

21 And the people said unto Joshua, Nay; but we will serve the LORD.

VER. 15. *Choose you this day whom ye will serve.* A most forcible irony. Would they take the gods of Mesopotamia, or the gods of Canaan? — which? The former their fathers had abandoned, the latter had not preserved their worshippers. As for Joshua, he would serve Jehovah.

VER. 18. The people adopt both premise and conclusion from Joshua.

VER. 19–21. Joshua strengthens the action of the people, by showing God's holy jealousy against all apostasy.

22 And Joshua said unto the people, Ye *are* witnesses against yourselves that ye have chosen you the LORD, to serve him. And they said, *We are* witnesses.

23 Now therefore put away (*said he*) the strange gods which *are* among you, and incline your heart unto the LORD God of Israel.

24 And the people said unto Joshua, The LORD our God will we serve, and his voice will we obey.

25 So Joshua made a covenant with the people that day, and set them a statute and an ordinance in Shechem.

26 ¶ And Joshua wrote these words in the book of the law of God, and took a great stone, and set it up there under an oak that *was* by the sanctuary of the LORD.

VER. 22–24. A final clinching of the solemn contract of the people. The third blow (as it were), to make all fast.

VER. 25. *So Joshua made a covenant.* Lit., " and Joshua cut a covenant." After the oral promises reiterated once and again, the ceremonies of a formal covenant are performed.

Statute and ordinance. A hendiadys for " a solemn sentence written or inscribed," probably cut into the great stone that was set up. (See next verse.)

VER. 26. Joshua added this record to the Pentateuch.

Under an oak that was by the sanctuary of the Lord. Rather, " under *the* oak that was in the sanctuary of Jehovah." That is, under the oak grove (or terebinth grove), where Abraham and Jacob had built their altars (see on ver. 1), and

27 And Joshua said unto all the people, Behold, this stone shall be a witness unto us; for it hath heard all the words of the LORD which he spake unto us: it shall be therefore a witness unto you, lest ye deny your God.

28 So Joshua let the people depart, every man unto his inheritance.

29 ¶ And it came to pass after these things. that Joshua the son of Nun the servant of the LORD died, *being* an hundred and ten years old.

30 And they buried him in the border of his inheritance in Timnath-serah, which *is* in mount Ephraim, on the north side of the hill of Gaash.

31 And Israel served the LORD all the days of Joshua, and all the days of the elders that overlived Joshua, and which had known all the works of the LORD that he had done for Israel.

32 ¶ And the bones of Joseph, which the children of Israel brought up out of Egypt, buried they in Shechem, in a parcel of ground which Jacob bought of the sons of Hamor the father of Shechem for an hundred pieces of silver; and it became the inheritance of the children of Joseph.

where Jacob had purified his family. This was "the sanctuary of Jehovah" in Shechem.

VER. 27. *It hath heard.* Compare, for this bold figure, Hab. ii. 11, and our Saviour's own words, Luke xix. 40.

VER. 30. *Timnath-serah.* (See on chap. xix. 50.)

The hill of Gaash is not identified. It is probably the hill of Deir Abu Meshal.

VER. 32. The burial of Joseph's bones, though mentioned here to save interrupting the story of Joshua, yet was doubtless made so soon as Israel gained possession of the soil.

Which Jacob bought. (See Gen. xxxiii. 19.)

33 And Eleazar the son of Aaron died; and they buried him in a hill *that pertained to* Phinehas his son, which was given him in mount Ephraim.

VER. 33. *In a hill that pertained to Phinehas.* Rather, " in Gibeath Phinehas," a place so called from his son. Perhaps it is the present *Jibia*, near the central Gilgal.

APPENDIX.

I. THE CHRONOLOGICAL QUESTION.

THE date in 1 Ki. vi. 1, is one of great importance in arranging any system of Old Testament chronology. We are there told that from the exodus to Solomon's accession there were four hundred and seventy-six years. Solomon's accession can be very proximately timed by the notices of reigns between his own and the destruction of Jerusalem by Nebuchadnezzar, where by the help of Babylonian and the later Persian records all is made plain. According to these data, Usher's date of 1015 for Solomon's accession is quite correct, and hence the year of the exodus would be B.C. 1491. Now this date would make the exodus to have occurred in the reign of Thotmes III. of Egypt, according to the Egyptian chronology of Wilkinson and others. But this hinge passage in 1 Kings is supposed to be an interpolation, from the fact that Origen quotes the passage immediately following, but omits this, and from the additional fact that Josephus and the early Christian historians seem not to have known it. Now if we take away the date in 1 Kings, we are left to two courses : either to go with Brugsch, and *lessen* the time between the exodus and Solomon, putting the exodus in the reign of Merneptah, son of the great Rameses (B.C. 1289– 1269) ; or to heed the *almost* necessity of the chronology of the Book of Judges, and *lengthen* the time between the exodus and Solomon, putting the exodus back in the seventeenth dynasty (B.C. 1651–1580*). We thus have a range of four hundred years, with regard to which we are in uncertainty as to the right place of the exodus. A difficulty of the first two dates has been suggested in the fact that the times immediately after Thotmes III. and Merneptah were so prosperous and warlike in Egyptian affairs as scarcely to permit the conquest of Canaan by Joshua. The last date might suit in this particular, if we accept the shorter Egyptian chronology, and put the exodus in the latter part of the seventeenth dynasty; but we use the longer chronology of Lepsius, we are then, if with our longer Israelitish chronology, only brought back to Thotmes III., and meet the old difficulty. Thus two hypotheses bring us to Thotmes, and it may be best to hold provisionally his date for the exodus, and to take Canon Cook's ingenious explanation of the difficulty. (See Speaker's Commentary, vol. i. pp. 459, 460.) In the progress of Egyptian discovery, we may hereafter find more solid data than any we now have.

If we take the whole of the disputed period of four hundred years from (say) B.C. 1660–1260, we find that the Chaldean kingdom made no impression upon the Palestine region during it, for the temporary raiding sway of Chedorlaomer was long before, and that of Chushan-risha-thaim (if he be Chaldean) was afterward. We find, also, that the Assyrian monarchy during these centuries had not ventured its strength beyond the Euphrates. Egypt was the only great kingdom that could have interfered with the progress of Israel to Canaan and its peaceful settle-

---

* This is Wilkinson's data; Lepsius and Brugsch make it 1706 B.C., one hundred and twenty-six years earlier, and so give an earlier date to Rameses than Wilkinson's years above.

ment; and from the fact that no mention of Egypt is made in the whole narrative, and no hostile attack of Egypt is noted till Rehoboam's day, five centuries after the exodus, we may conclude that Egypt adopted the policy of leaving Israel untouched in her frequent invasions of Syria during the eighteenth, nineteenth, twentieth, and twenty-first dynasties. This may have been a policy of the great empire (providentially ordered by God for the protection of his people), by which to put a barrier between the Rutennu and Cheta on the north and Egypt on the south. Such an hypothesis would explain the wonderful security of Israel for centuries, while so near their old and powerful oppressor in the height of its grandeur. Certainly, it is a most marvellous fact that from Israel we hear nothing of Egypt for five centuries, in which such monarchs as Thotmes III., Amenotep II. and III., Seti, Rameses I., II., and III., were overrunning western Asia. This is perhaps one of the strongest arguments for putting the exodus at a late date, just before the depressed state of Egypt which seems to have followed the reign of Rameses III. Yet strong as it is, it is too solidly met by the demand for a much longer time between the exodus and Solomon for us to accept it, and we therefore fall back upon our hypothesis, above stated, for the non-appearance of Egypt in Israelitish history between the time of the Pharaoh of the exodus and Shishak.

II. THE MIRACLES.

The grand miracles of the dividing of the Jordan, the fall of Jericho's walls, and the standing still of the sun and moon, have received an unusual share of infidel attack. They really formed part of the same series of miracles which began with the plagues of Egypt, and was contin-·

ued in the dividing of the Red Sea, the guidance of the cloud, and the daily furnishing of the manna. It was the period of founding a great church by the God of Salvation, and he surrounded its founding with glorious evidences, as afterward he surrounded the founding of the Christian Church, its development, with like miraculous evidences for the conviction of mankind. We should look just to such epochs as those in which marvels from God's hand should be dealt out to the world. That a miracle is impossible, is an absurdity to any mind that believes in God, and, if possible, then here is just the place for miracles. Further, that a miracle cannot be proved by evidence, is an absurdity to any one who believes in man. If men are good witnesses to a steamer's explosion, they are equally good witnesses to a rapid river ceasing its flow for several hours, and then resuming its fulness and force. As to the miracles of the Book of Joshua, the evidence for each is the same; and yet it is strange how many who accept the miracle of the Jordan and of Jericho, hesitate at the sun's standing still, and endeavor to explain it away. They say it is poetry. But if it be poetry, it is quoted as history by the sacred historian in a most matter-of-fact narrative. To introduce a mere flight of poetry in such a narrative would be not only awkward but false. But, beside this, no poetry would dare to make a mere wish of Joshua's, or a retrospective rejoicing of Israel, take the form of this quotation from the Book of Jasher; thus (Josh. x. 12–14), "Then spake Joshua to Jehovah in the day when Jehovah delivered up the Amorites before the children of Israel, and he said in the sight of Israel, Sun, stand thou still upon Gibeon, and thou, Moon, in the valley of Ajalon. And the sun stood still, and the moon stayed, until the people had avenged themselves upon their enemies. Is not this written in the book of Jasher? So the sun stood still in the midst of heaven, and hasted not to go down about a whole day. And there was no day like that before it or after it, that Jehovah hearkened unto the voice of a man : for Jehovah fought for Israel." Surely if the sun and moon continued their apparent courses, this would be poetry run mad. The quotation from Deborah's triumphant song is often used as a parallel, " The stars in their courses fought against Sisera," but this would be a perfectly legitimate hyperbole for the shrouding of the stars in darkness, by which God may have made the night too dark for successful flight. The detailed statements of our passage in Joshua bear no comparison with this poetry of Deborah. But still further, it is highly improbable that the passage, after the mention of the Book of Jasher, is either quotation or poetry. It is rather the sacred historian's comment on the quotation, and his repetition of its main truth. .

The argument against the miracle, that it is never again mentioned, has no force whatever, even were it true, for many wonderful manifestations of God's power are mentioned but once. But it is not true, for in Hab. iii. 11, the reference to this event is unmistakable.

As to the miracle itself, no one for a moment would suppose that a literal standing still of sun and moon is necessarily intended. To argue from this phraseology, that it shows an ignorance of astronomy, and is therefore a part of a false record, is puerile, and should be so held by every one who says " the sun rises " and " the sun sets." There was an *apparent* stoppage of the apparent courses of the sun and moon, whether by action through the laws of refraction or otherwise it matters little. God could do it, that's enough. This apparent stoppage of sun and

moon occurred early in the day, as the sun stood still over
Gibeon, and the army of Joshua was at the west of that
city.　This shows that the ordinary reason for the miracle
(that the day should be prolonged and give more time for
the pursuit) is incorrect.　The miracle was wrought early
in the day, probably as an encouragement to Israel, to
whom it was announced by Joshua as a sign of Jehovah's
presence and blessing.　The stoppage may have continued
only a few hours, long enough to serve its purpose as a
divine sign.　The phrase, "hasted not to go down about
a whole day," does not militate against this view, for that
passage, strictly rendered, should read, "hasted not to go
down as a perfect day," *i.e.*, tarried, and did not hurry on,
as it does on every ordinary day.

III. The Moral Question.

The cruelty of the destruction of the Canaanites has
been always emphasized by the opponents of the Scriptures,
and has been one of the most plausible arguments against
revelation.　The manner in which the objection is put is
this: that the slaughter by the Israelites of hundreds of
thousands of innocent children and women, as well as men
in arms, in order to clear a land for the settlement of
themselves, is a piece of selfishness and barbarism not to be
equalled by any fact in the history of violence and rapacity,
and that such conduct could never have been sanctioned by
a just and holy God, but must have received his righteous
reprobation; hence any mark of God's approval as here
recorded is a falsehood, and the whole history is proved to
be a fraud.　This specious reasoning is very apt to carry
away a superficial thinker, because its parts hold well
together, and you vainly strive to find a weak link in the
chain.　If the statement be true, the conclusion is irresist-

ible. But it is in the statement the treachery lies. The Israelites did not slaughter women and children *in order to clear a land for themselves*, but they did it *in order to be faithful to God.* The act was not theirs at all, but God's; and they even resisted its performance, and spared the Canaanites again and again, in opposition to the divine commandment. God had ordered the extermination of the Canaanites at their hand, both directing it to be fully done, in spite of their promptings to spare, and also declaring that the judgment upon Canaan had nothing to do with Israel's superiority or any right on Israel's part (Deut. vii. 2, xx. 16–18, as compared with ver. 10, also Deut. ix. 4–6). We are therefore to consider Israel as an obedient instrument in God's hand, and view the action as entirely God's. This takes it out of the analogy of human actions, and prohibits our condemning verdict. Are we ready to condemn God for causing the death of women and children? Are we ready to blame him for using the pestilence, the wasting fever, the racking pains of inflammation and rheumatism, in dissolving the human body? What are we, that we can enter into the counsels of the Most High, and act the critic there? Does it not become us to be dumb and submissive, confiding in his infinite truth? This is the state of the question. God is not sanctioning cruelty in man by this exceptional action through Israel any more than the State is sanctioning cruelty in man by its charge to the sheriff for the execution of a thousand criminals. God especially fortified Israel against receiving a taste or tendency for cruelty from these peculiar circumstances by the merciful provisions of the Mosaic law, and the careful details of the religious life of the nation. The people were watched over with the assiduity and constant provision of a nurse with her child, and could thus be safely entrusted with a commission which to other nations would have been injurious. The above reasoning would hold good if every Canaanite had been destroyed; but the instance of Rahab reveals a principle of exception that must not be overlooked. The depraved people of Palestine had for forty years been warned of the coming judgments, and called to the true God by the events occurring almost at their doors. The grand evidences of Jehovah's presence and will in the plagues of Egypt, the parting of the Red Sea, the guidance of the cloud, and the daily supply of manna, were well known to all the tribes of Canaan. God was near them, and coming toward them to punish them, and in his mercy he gave them forty years to turn unto him. But all this warning display of the Divine purpose produced in the Canaanites (as such long-suffering threatenings are wont to do with wilful man) a strange mingling of fear and resistance, instead of penitence and faith. Rahab, however, was an instance of the penitence and faith, and her statement throws great light on the whole subject of Canaan's warning. It is this: " I know that Jehovah hath given you the land, and that your terror is fallen upon us, and that all the inhabitants of the land faint because of you ; for we have heard how the Lord dried up the water of the Red Sea for you, when ye came out of Egypt [i.e., forty years before]; and what ye did unto the two kings of the Amorites that were on the other side Jordan, Sihon and Og, whom ye utterly destroyed [i.e., only the preceding year]. And as soon as we had heard these things, our hearts did melt, neither did there remain any more courage in any man, because of you; for Jehovah your God, he is God in heaven above and in earth beneath " (Josh. ii. 9–11). How many of Canaan's inhabitants acted as Rahab, and were spared, we know not. There may have been thousands. But we know this additional fact of God's mercy amid his righteous judgments, that Rahab's faith in Jehovah secured from Canaan's fate not only herself, but her father and mother, her brothers and sisters, and all belonging to their families ("all that they have," chap. ii. 13 ; "all her kindred," chap. vi. 23). The Mosaic system, which made ample provision for the stranger as well as the Hebrew, may have embraced in Palestine many thousands of these believing and spared Canaanites.

IV. THE SPIRITUAL LESSONS OF THE BOOK.

The book is a grand lesson of trust in a covenant Jehovah, whose strength is assured to his people. It shows his tenderness at the same time with his holy severity against wanton disregard of his commandments. Presumptuous Achan is cut off, but Israel, failing to destroy the Canaanites, not from presumptuousness, but from lack of faith and courage, is not cut off, but is plagued by its own weakness. The power of a pure piety to cement brethren together is also demonstrated in this story of Israel's purest period, and the relation of the two (love to God and love to the brethren) is beautifully illustrated in the action and reaction between the tribes touching the altar-monument erected by the trans-Jordanic tribes in the Jordan valley. Everywhere in the book the ritual is shown to be subservient to the spiritual, and the service of God is the obedient heart and the loving devotion of the whole man. In God's words to Joshua, in Achan's sad story, in the scene at Ebal, in the parting of the trans-Jordanic tribes, and in the two valedictories of Joshua, the deep heart-religion of the Mosaic system is especially evident.

Nor can we ignore the lessons that come to us through a symbolism which we are taught by the Apostle Paul and the author of the Epistle to the Hebrews. We see, not as a poetic imagination, but as a heavenly instruction, the entrance into Canaan symbolizing the believer's entrance into rest, not the rest of heaven, but the rest which even here he has in Jesus Christ. We see that in this rest he may be disturbed by his own lack of faith, the results of which failure will be thorns in his side, and that only by a complete commitment of himself to the will of God will his rest be made perfect. We see, moreover, how our Joshua (Jesus) is the sole guide to this rest, so that as Jesus is both priest and sacrifice, both foundation and builder, so is he both the Rest and the Guide to it.

In the light of the New Testament, this book of Joshua will prove full of spiritual comfort and edification to every seeking believer. God has placed it in the canon not to praise Joshua or Israel, but to teach and bless his dear people to the end of time.

Cambridge: Press of John Wilson and Son.

BIBLE HELPS,

PUBLISHED BY

ROBERT CARTER & BROTHERS,

No. 530 BROADWAY, NEW YORK.

———◆———

Jacobus on Genesis	$1.50
Jacobus on Exodus. Vol. I.	1.00
Dr. Crosby on Joshua	1.50
Dr. Green on Job	1.75
Horne on the Psalms	2.50
Bridges on the Proverbs	2.50
Hamilton on Ecclesiastes. (Royal Preacher)	1.25
Newton on the Song of Solomon	1 25
Jacobus on the Gospels. 2 vols.	3.00
Ryle on the Gospels. 7 vols.	10.50
Bonar on the Gospels	2.00
Jacobus on the Acts	1.50
Bonar on the Acts	2.00
Haldane on Romans	3 00
Chalmers on Romans	2.50
Brown on Romans	2.00
Hodge on Corinthians. 2 vols.	3.50
Hodge on Ephesians	1.75
Lillie on Thessalonians	2.00
Sampson on Hebrews	3.00
Newton on Hebrews	1 50
Bonar on Revelation	2.00

———

Horne's Introduction to the Bible	5.00
Henry's Commentary. 9 vols., $27.00 5 vols.	25.00
Pool's Annotations on the Bible. 3 vols.	15.00
Kitto's Bible Illustrations. 4 vols.	7 00
Dr. Hanna's Life of Christ. 3 vols.	4 50
Fraser's Synoptical Lectures on the Bible. 2 vols.	4.00
The Book and Its Story	1.50
Fresh Leaves from the Book and Its Story	2.00
Brown on the Discourses and Sayings of our Lord	3.50
Bowes, The Scripture its own Illustrator	1.50
Drummond on the Parables	1.75
Dykes on the Sermon on the Mount. 3 vols.	3 75
The Word Series. By Miss Warner. 3 vols.	4 50
The Footsteps of St. Paul. By Macduff.	1.50

530 Broadway, New York,
November, 1874.

ROBERT CARTER & BROTHERS'

NEW BOOKS.

───◆───

EXPOSITORY NOTES ON JOSHUA. By Howard Crosby, D.D. 12mo. $1.00.

An admirable book for teachers pursuing the International Series of Lessons which, on January, 1875, enter upon the book of Joshua.

THE SCOTTISH PHILOSOPHY. Biographical, Expository, and Critical. By James McCosh, D.D., LL.D., President of Princeton College. 8vo. $4.00.

From the Preface.

"The English-speaking public, British and American, has been listening to divers forms of philosophy, — to Coleridge, to Kant, to Cousin, to Hegel, to Comte, to Berkeley, — and is now inclined to a materialistic psychology. Not finding permanent satisfaction in any of these, it is surely possible that it may grant a hearing to the sober philosophy of Scotland.

"I have tried to make my work a contribution to what may be regarded as a new department of science, the history of thought, which is quite as important as the history of wars, of commerce, of literature, or of civilization."

CHRISTIAN THEOLOGY FOR THE PEOPLE. By Willis Lord, D.D., LL.D. 8vo. $4.00.

"Our theology has long needed some popular and attractive dress like this. Most of the old treatises on Systematic Theology are too long, too learned, too heavy as to style, too much in the form of lectures and sermons. Dr. Lord has steered clear of all these faults. He has produced a work comprehensive as a whole, attractive in form, brief in each particular part, sound in doctrine, true to Scripture. evangelical in spirit, beautiful in diction, which any intelligent layman, or any intelligent lady, not less than our ministers and students of divinity, might read with profit and delight. To all such, who wish to know what our theology is, we heartily commend it." — *Interior.*

CHRISTIANITY AND SCIENCE: A Series of Lectures by the Rev. A. P. Peabody, D.D., of Harvard College. 12mo. $1.75.

This volume, uniform with Dr. McCosh's "Christianity and Positivism," is, like Dr. McCosh's work, a series of lectures on the Ely Foundation of the Union Theological Seminary. At the close of the last of the lectures. Dr. John Hall (as reported in the "New York Observer") said: "I will venture to tell the young men who enjoyed these lectures that, when they wish for a type and model of calm, dispassionate argument, of transparent style through which the meaning shines, of eloquence that is not aware that it is eloquence. of beauty that does not show itself beautiful, they have only to look back, as I shall long do with pleasure, on this course by Dr. Peabody."

BY THE AUTHOR OF THE "WIDE WIDE WORLD."

A Series of Tales illustrative of the Lord's Prayer.

1. THE LITTLE CAMP ON EAGLE HILL. A Tale. Illustrating the Introduction to the Lord's Prayer. 16mo. $1.25.

"The exquisite spiritual lessons, which are mingled with the making of hemlock beds and cooking of fish, will cause some who are no longer children to linger lovingly over its pages." — *Weekly Witness.*

2. WILLOW BROOK. A Tale. Illustrative of the First Petition of the Lord's Prayer. 16mo. $1.25.

"In her own inimitable style of easy, natural, and cheery dialogue, with never-ending interest in every-day matters. 'Willow Brook' is a pleasant story that keeps up unflagging attention by its vivacity and variety, and edifies by its moral and religious tone." — *Ladies' Repository.*

3. SCEPTRES AND CROWNS. A Tale. Illustrative of the Second Petition of the Lord's Prayer. 16mo. $1.25.

"The story is simply and often sweetly told, intermingled with religious conversations that bring out the great truths of the Gospel and the lessons of personal duty, while the entertaining element is by no means wanting."—*Evangelist.*

4. THE FLAG OF TRUCE. A Tale. Illustrative of the Third Petition of the Lord's Prayer. 16mo. $1.25.

"Miss Warner's works never wait long for buyers or readers. She has won her way to so many hearts, that her successive productions are commended by all the pleasant memories they have awakened in the grateful homes they have visited." — *Christian at Work.*

A STORY OF SMALL BEGINNINGS. Containing "What She Could," "Opportunities," "House in Town," and "Trading." By the Author of the "Wide Wide World." 4 vols. In a box. $5.00.

"Miss Warner has a remarkable facility in the collection of charming little books for the young people, and the present work is no exception to the rule. She takes her heroine from a life of toil and dependence, and places her amid luxury and temptation, yet, with the Bible in her hand, she conquers them all." — *Journal.*

THE WONDER CASE. By the Rev. R. NEWTON, D.D. Containing: —

BIBLE WONDERS	. . . . $1.25	LEAVES FROM TREE OF LIFE.	$1.25
NATURE'S WONDERS	. . . 1.25	RILLS FROM FOUNTAIN	. . . 1.25
JEWISH TABERNACLE	. . . 1.25	GIANTS AND WONDERS	. . . 1.25

6 *vols. In a box.* $7.50.

THE JEWEL CASE. By the Same. 6 vols. In a box. $7.50.

"Dr. Newton possesses the rare faculty of writing successfully for the young. He interests, instructs, and benefits them at once. His style is clear and simple, but not childish; and it is a pleasure for children of all ages — from ten to fourscore — to read his books, which have attained such a wide popularity in this country and Europe." — *Lutheran Observer.*

GOLDEN APPLES. Fit Words for the Young. By the Rev EDGAR WOODS. 16mo. $1.00.

"Many a mother will be pleased to possess it, that she may, by its aid, be able to make her little ones acquainted with the teachings of the Master." - *Baptist Union.*

FOLLOW THE LAMB; or, Counsels to Converts. By HORATIUS BONAR, D.D. 18mo. 40 cents.

"There is a great deal of wisdom compressed in this little book, and it would be well if a copy were placed in the hands of every beginner in the Christian life." — *Albany Evening Journal.*

EARTH'S MORNING; or, Thoughts on Genesis. By HORATIUS BONAR, D.D.

THE RENT VEIL. By HORATIUS BONAR, D.D.

CLEFTS IN THE ROCK; or, The Believer's Ground of Confidence in Christ. By the Rev. J. R. MACDUFF, D.D. 16mo. $1.50.

The author of "Memories of Bethany," and of "Morning and Night Watches," has secured for himself an honorable place among the writers of devotional books.

THE WHITE ROSE OF LANGLEY. A Tale. By EMILY SARAH HOLT. $1.50.

The author of this volume has admirable talent for grouping in charming narrative the facts of history, and this is one of her most interesting books

BY THE SAME AUTHOR.

1. **VERENA.** A Tale of To-day. $1.50.

2. **ISOULT BARRY, OF WYNSCOTE.** A Tale of Tudor Times. By EMILY SARAH HOLT. $1.50.

3. **ROBIN TREMAYNE.** A Tale of the Marian Persecution. A Sequel to the above. $1.50.

"The advent of Fronde, Burke, and others, as lecturers on Irish and English history, have imparted a new interest to the study of English history, especially of the period of the Tudors; and it is fortunate for American readers that there should have appeared, just at this time, two narratives of Tudor times — 'Isoult Barry, of Wynscote,' and 'Robin Tremayne' — which, in their careful record of the events of those times, their fidelity to the manners, customs, and language of the period, and their skilful limning of the prominent actors, both princes and nobles, throw more light upon the era of the Tudor dynasty than any merely historical work could possibly do." — *Educational Monthly.*

4. **ASHCLIFFE HALL.** A Tale of the Last Century. $1.25.

"Deserves a high place among the best books of its class. It is both well written and thoroughly entertaining from beginning to end " — *Record.*

5. **THE WELL IN THE DESERT.** An Old Legend of the House of Arundel. $1 25.

"A tale of the Middle Ages, showing that there were beautiful gleams of light even in those dark days. It is a touching story." — *The Christian.*

Lightning Source UK Ltd.
Milton Keynes UK
UKHW040217080121
376598UK00002BA/587

9 783348 023382